SCIENCE WORKSHOP SERIES

BIOLOGY

Dynamic Processes

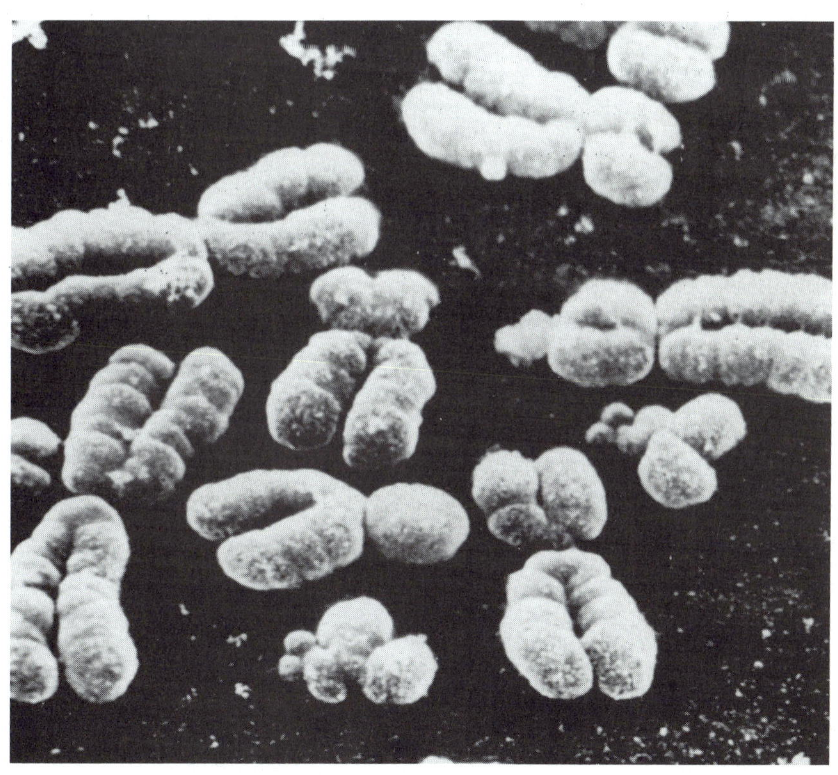

Seymour Rosen

GLOBE BOOK COMPANY
A Division of Simon & Schuster
Englewood Cliffs, New Jersey

THE AUTHOR

Seymour Rosen received his B.A. and M.S. degrees from Brooklyn College. He taught science in the New York City School System for twenty-seven years. Mr. Rosen was also a contributing participant in a teacher-training program for the development of science curriculum for the New York City Board of Education.

Cover Photograph: Biophoto Associates/Science Source
Photo Researcher: Rhoda Sidney

Photo Credits:

p. 10, Fig. D: Runk/Schoenberger, Grant Heilman
p. 34: Alan Carey/The Image Works
p. 61, Fig. A: National Audubon Society/Photo Researchers
p. 61, Fig. B: Hal Harrison/Grant Heilman
p. 62, Fig. C: Christian Grzimek/Photo Researchers
p. 62, Fig. D: National Audubon Society/Photo Researchers
p. 82, Fig. C: Peter Menzel/Stock, Boston
p. 94: Heilman/Monkmeyer Press Photos
p. 115, Fig. H: PhotoTrends
p. 116, Fig. I: Rhoda Sidney
p. 123, Fig. F: Communicable Disease Center
p. 123, Fig. G: Christopher Morrow/Stock, Boston
p. 144, Fig. B: Grant Heilman
p. 144, Fig. C: National Audubon Society/Photo Researchers
p. 144, Fig. D: Carl Frank, Photo Researchers
p. 144, Fig. E: Lee Snider, Photo Images
p. 145, Fig. F: Omikron/Photo Researchers
p. 145, Fig. G: Fredrik D. Bodin/Stock, Boston
p. 155, Fig. A: United Nations
p. 155, Fig. B: Runk/Schoenberger/Grant Heilman
p. 158: Peter Menzel/Stock, Boston
p. 161, Fig. A: Bethlehem Steel Corporation
p. 162, Fig. C: Photo Researchers
p. 163, Fig. E: Photo Researchers
p. 163, Fig. F: Advertising Council, U.S.D.A. Forest Service
p. 164, Fig. G: Grant Heilman
p. 164, Fig. H: Wendell Metzen/Bruce Coleman

ISBN: 0-8359-0374-5

Printed in the United States of America
4 5 6 7 8 9 10 95 94

Globe Book Company
A Division of Simon & Schuster
Englewood Cliffs, New Jersey

CONTENTS

GENETICS

EVOLUTION

VIRUSES AND DISEASE

ECOLOGY

Introduction to Dynamic Processes

Has anyone ever told you that you have your mother's eyes? What did they mean? In this book, you will learn about the close similarities between parents and their offspring. Offspring resemble their parents because they inherit certain traits, or characteristics from them. You will learn the reasons why you may resemble either of your parents.

You also will learn about evolution, or the process by which organisms change over time. We will trace the path of theories of evolution from the time of Charles Darwin to present day theories.

In this book, you also will learn about viruses and disease. The difference between infectious disease and noninfectious disease will be explained. In addition, ways of preventing diseases, such as AIDS will be discussed.

Finally, you will learn more about ecology and conservation and what you can do to make the environment a better place in which to live.

What are traits?

1

traits: characteristics of living things

LESSON 1 | What are traits?

It is easy to recognize an elephant. An elephant is very large and has a long trunk. A giraffe is easy to recognize too—by its long neck.

The elephant's trunk and the giraffe's neck are examples of **traits**. Traits are characteristics that living things have. They help us to identify living things.

Scientists have divided living things into groups according to traits. All members of a group have certain traits that are the same. For example, all birds have feathers. All mammals have some hair. All giraffes have long necks. And all elephants are large and have long trunks.

Organisms within a group may share certain traits, but no two are exactly alike. There are always individual differences. We call these differences individual traits.

Take the elephant for example. All elephants are large, but some are larger than others. All giraffes have long necks, but some giraffes have longer necks than others.

All humans share certain traits. However, no two people are exactly alike—not even identical twins. There are always individual differences.

Individual differences enable us to identify different members of the same group.

Think of your friends, for example. You know one from another by their individual traits. They include differences in size, hair type and coloring, skin coloring, and shape of face. How many other human traits can you name?

IDENTIFYING LIVING THINGS BY GROUP TRAITS

Figure A

Humans and frogs are alike in some ways. They share certain traits. For example:

- Both humans and frogs are living things. Therefore, both carry out the life processes.
- Both humans and frogs are animals.
- Both humans and frogs are vertebrates. They have backbones.

But humans and frogs are different from one another too—very different. We can tell humans from frogs by the traits they do not share.

Fifteen traits are listed below and on the next page. Some are human traits. Some are traits that frogs have.

Study each trait. Does it belong to humans or does it belong to frogs? Write Human next to each human trait. Write Frog next to each frog trait.

1. some hair covering ______________

2. external fertilization ______________

3. internal fertilization ______________

4. embryos develop outside the female's body ______________

5. females can nurse their young ______________

6. give birth to live young ______________

7. live entire life on land ______________

8. live early part of life in water and adult life on land ______________

9. breathe by lungs only ______________

10. breathe through gills in early life ______________

11. adults breathe by lungs or through skin ______________

12. stand on two legs ______________

13. stand on four legs ______________

14. eat only insects ______________

15. eat meat and plants ______________

Now answer these questions.

16. Do all humans have the traits you have listed as "Human"? ______________

17. Do all frogs have the traits you have listed as "Frog"? ______________

18. The traits you have listed are all ______________ traits.
group, individual

19. Are all frogs exactly alike? ______________

20. Are all humans exactly alike? ______________

IDENTIFYING INDIVIDUALS BY INDIVIDUAL TRAITS

Look at Figure B and then answer the questions.

John, Jim, and Tom are humans. They are about the same age. They have all the traits that humans share. Yet, they are different from one another.

Figure B

- John is short and thin. He has light-brown skin and dark straight hair.
- Jim is tall and heavy. He has dark-brown skin and dark curly hair.
- Tom is tall and thin. He has fair skin and light curly hair.

1. Identify by letter.

   a) Which one is John? ________________

   b) Which one is Jim? ________________

   c) Which one is Tom? ________________

2. a) Do all humans have hair? ________________

   b) Hair ________________ a human trait.
   is, is not

   c) Do all humans have the same color hair? ________________

   d) Do all humans have curly hair? ________________

   e) Do all humans have straight hair? ________________

3. What kind of trait is hair color and type? ________________
   individual, group

4. At a given age, is every person the same height? ________________

5. Are some people taller than average? ________________

6. Are some people shorter than average? ________________

7. Difference in height is what kind of trait? ________________
   individual, group

Figure C shows two pea pods and their peas. Both are the same age.

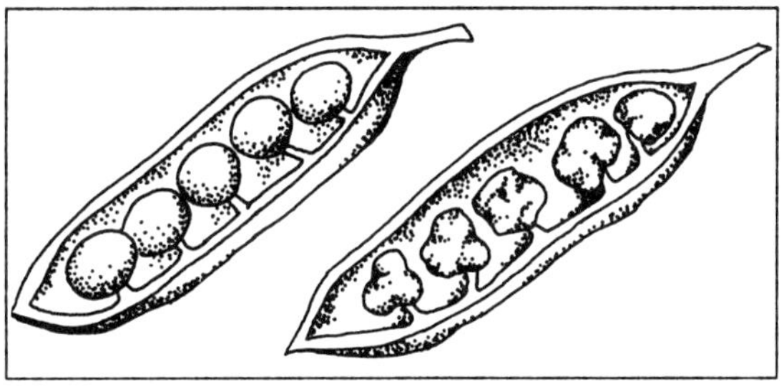

8. Are the peas of these pods exactly the same? ________________

9. What difference do you notice in the skins of the peas?

   ____

   ____

Figure C

10. What kind of difference is this? ________________
    individual, group

FILL IN THE BLANK

Complete each statement using a term or terms from the list below. Write your answers in the spaces provided.

group	the same	plants
traits	individual traits	exactly
humans	individual	identified
living things		

1. The characteristics a living thing has are called ______________ .
2. Living things are ______________ by their traits.
3. Scientists group ______________ according to their traits.
4. Members of a group have certain traits that are ______________ .
5. No two living things are ______________ the same.
6. Difference among individuals of the same group are called ______________ .
7. Having a spinal cord, internal fertilization and embryo development are group traits of ______________ .
8. Individual differences enable us to identify different members of the same ______________ .
9. Having cell walls and making their own food are group traits of ______________ .
10. Wrinkled skin or smooth skin are ______________ traits of peas.

MATCHING

Match each term in Column A with its description in Column B. Write the correct letter in the space provided.

	Column A	Column B
________	**1.** traits	**a)** group trait of birds
________	**2.** feathers	**b)** individual human trait
________	**3.** color of feathers	**c)** human group trait
________	**4.** hair	**d)** characteristics
________	**5.** hair texture	**e)** individual trait of birds

What are chromosomes? 2

chromosome [KROH-muh-sohm]: threadlike structures in the nucleus of a cell that control heredity
gamete: sex cell
gene: part of a chromosome that controls inherited traits
genetics [juh-NET-iks]: study of heredity

LESSON 2 | What are chromosomes?

"Mary has her mother's eyes." "Tom is built just like his father." How often have you heard remarks like these?

All people resemble their parents in some ways. They have similar traits. . . . And it is no accident. Many traits are passed on from parents to offspring. We say they are inherited. How are they inherited? The answer is found in the cell nucleus.

The nucleus has tiny bodies called **chromosomes** [KROH-muh-sohms]. Most are rod-shaped. In body cells, chromosomes are found in pairs. Body cells are all the cells except sperm and egg cells.

Each kind of organism has a specific number of chromosomes. For example, every body cell of a fruit fly has 8 chromosomes (4 pairs); a human has 46 (23 pairs); a garden pea has 14 (7 pairs).

Along each chromosome there are many dark bands. Each band is a small part of a chromosome called a **gene**. There are many, many genes, at least one million in every nucleus. Genes determine the traits of an organism.

There are genes for height, genes for nose size and shape, genes for the color of hair, skin, and eyes. In fact, there are genes for most traits any individual has. Some genes even affect traits like voice, intelligence and behavior. Genes also control the life processes of your cells.

In both asexual and sexual reproduction, chromosomes (and genes) are passed from parents to offspring. During asexual reproduction, each daughter cell receives chromosomes from a single parent cell. The daughter cell is an exact copy of the parent. Some organisms and the body cells of all organisms reproduce asexually.

During sexual reproduction, an offspring receives chromosomes from each parent cell. The chromosomes in **gametes**, or sex cells, are not paired. A sperm or an egg cell has only half the number of chromosomes as a body cell. When fertilization takes place, the sperm cell and the egg cell unite. Together, their chromosomes add up to the full number of chromosomes found in body cells. The fertilized egg, or zygote, has chromosomes from both of its parents. It also has traits from both parents.

CHROMOSOMES AND GENES

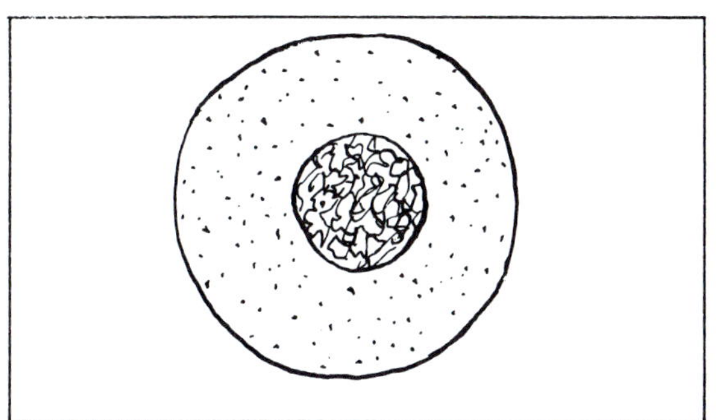

Figure A

Every cell has a nucleus.

1. Figure A shows an animal cell.

   a) Draw a line to the nucleus.

   b) Label it "nucleus."

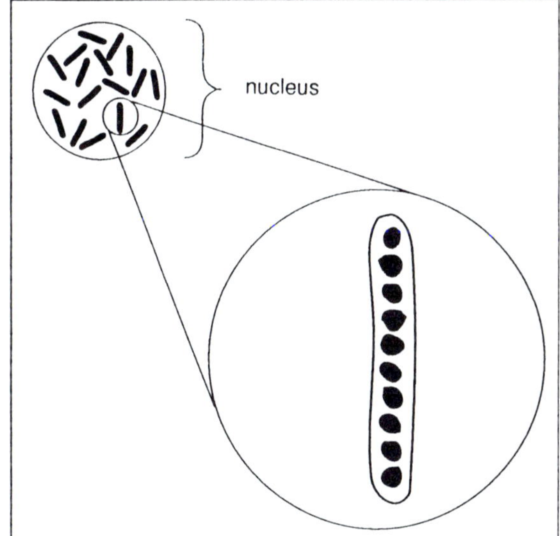

Figure B

2. A nucleus contains tiny rod-shaped bodies. What are they called?

   ____

3. A chromosome is made up of even smaller bodies. What are they called?

   ____

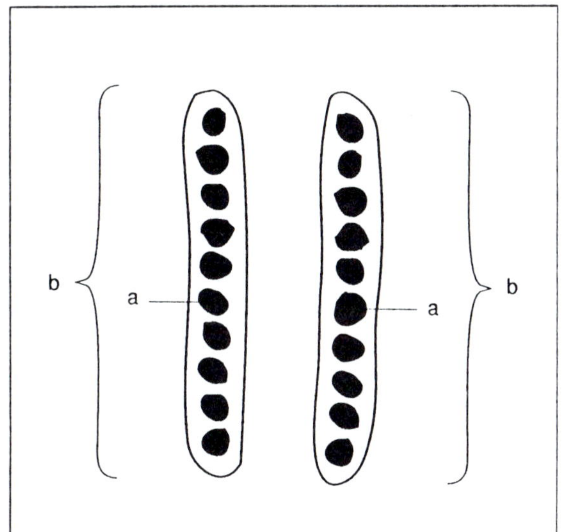

Figure C

4. Figure C shows a pair of chromosomes and their genes.

   a) The chromosomes are labeled

      ________ .

   b) Two genes are labeled ________ .

5. Why are genes important? ________

   ____

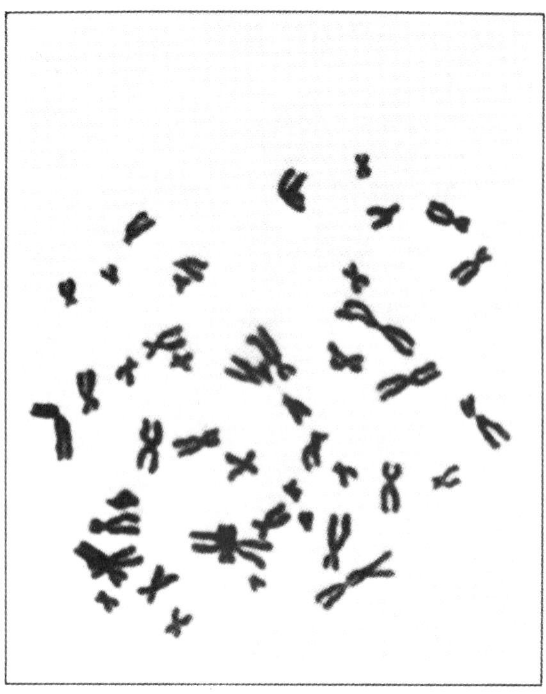

Figure D *Human chromosomes*

Figure D shows what actual human chromosomes look like.

- Every body cell of a particular organism has the same chromosomes.
- No two individuals that reproduce sexually have the same chromosomes.

You have trillions of body cells. Each cell has the same chromosomes. No one else in the world has the same chromosomes. There is no "duplicate" of you—anywhere!

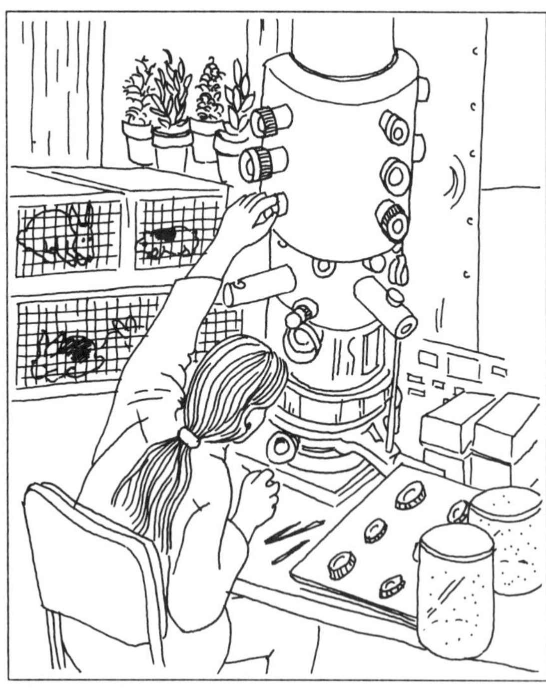

Figure E

The study of traits and how they are passed on is called **genetics** [juh-NET-iks].

- All living things have traits.
- All living things have genes.
- Only living things have genes.

Genes contain the "plans" for the traits an organism has.

What are genes made of? Scientists have discovered that genes are made of a complicated compound called DNA. DNA stands for deoxyribonucleic [dee-oks-ee-ry-boh-noo-KLEE-ik] acid. Try to pronounce it.

FILL IN THE BLANK

Complete each statement using a term or terms from the list below. Write your answers in the spaces provided. Some words may be used more than once.

genes	46	specific
pairs	genetics	23
inherited	traits	chromosomes

1. The characteristics an individual has are called ________________.
2. Traits are passed down from parents to offspring. Another way of saying this is "traits are ________________".
3. The study of heredity is called ________________.
4. The nucleus has tiny rod-shaped bodies called ________________.
5. A chromosome is made up of a chain of ________________.
6. Genes determine the ________________ of an individual.
7. Every organism has a ________________ number of chromosomes.
8. In body cells, chromosomes are found in ________________.
9. Each of your body cells has ________________ pairs of chromosomes. This is a total of ________________ single chromosomes.
10. A human sperm or egg has ________________ single chromosomes.

MATCHING

Match each term in Column A with its description in Column B. Write the correct letter in the space provided.

	Column A	Column B
________	**1.** genes	**a)** compound that makes up genes
________	**2.** chromosomes	**b)** made up of many genes
________	**3.** DNA	**c)** have unpaired chromosomes
________	**4.** body cells	**d)** pass on traits
________	**5.** gametes	**e)** have paired chromosomes

WHAT DO THE PICTURES SHOW?

The pictures below show how chromosomes are passed from parent to offspring during asexual and sexual reproduction. Study Figures F and G. Then answer the questions.

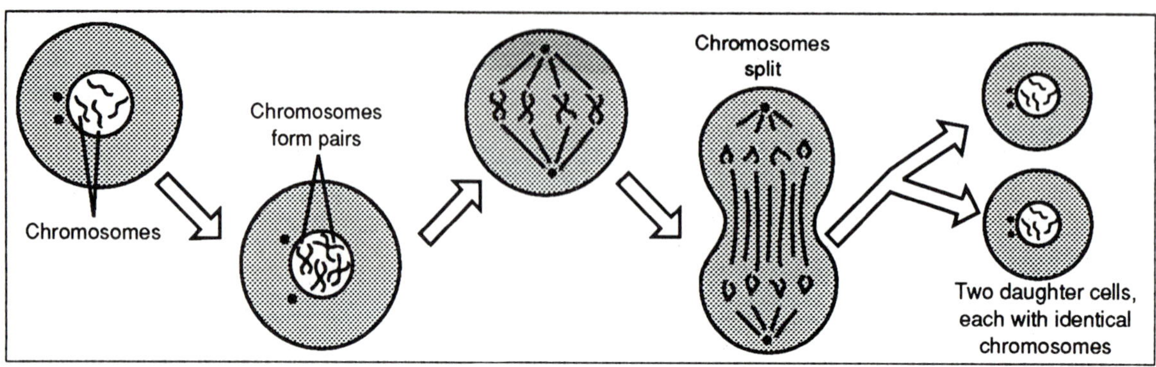

Figure F *Asexual reproduction*

1. How many chromosomes does the parent cell in Figure F have? ________
2. How many chromosomes does each daughter cell have? ________
3. In Figure F, how do the parent cell's chromosomes compare to the daughter cell's chromosomes? ________________________________
4. Which Figure shows how body cells reproduce? ________ F, G
5. a. In Figure G, how many chromosomes does each sperm cell contain? ________
   b. How many chromosomes does each egg cell contain? ________

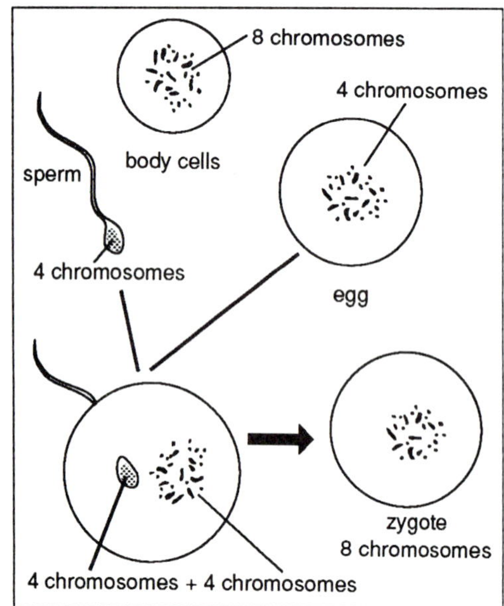

Figure G *Sexual reproduction*

6. Gametes have ____________ (half, twice) the number of chromosomes as body cells.
7. Fertilization produces a single cell. What is it called? ____________
8. How many chromosomes does the zygote in Figure G have? ____________
9. How many chromosomes will each body cell of the organism have? ____________
10. The offspring will have traits of both the mother and father. Why? ____________ ________________________________

NUMBER, PLEASE!

Fill in the missing number of chromosomes.

	Organism	Chromosomes in each body cell	Chromosomes in each sperm or egg
1.	Human	46	
2.	Horse	60	
3.	Housefly		6
4.	Dog	78	
5.	Grasshopper		7
6.	Mosquito		3
7.	Chicken	18	
8.	Apple		17
9.	Spinach	12	
10.	Lily		12

11. A gamete has ______________ the number of chromosomes that a body cell has.
half, twice

12. How many pairs of chromosomes are there in each body cell of the following?

a) horse ________

b) mosquito ________

c) spinach ________

d) lily ________

e) human ________

f) housefly ________

WORD SCRAMBLE

Below are several scrambled words you have used in this Lesson. Unscramble the words and write your answers in the spaces provided.

1. NEEG ______________________________

2. HERINIT ______________________________

3. NEGITECS ______________________________

4. ETEMAG ______________________________

5. CHOMEOSORM ______________________________

TRUE OR FALSE

In the space provided, write "true" if the sentence is true. Write "false" if the sentence is false.

________ 1. Traits are the characteristics of living things.

________ 2. Only animals have traits.

________ 3. Traits are passed on from offspring to parents.

________ 4. Traits are passed on by genes.

________ 5. A cell has only a few genes.

________ 6. Only animals have genes.

________ 7. Different genes control different traits.

________ 8. Genes form chromosomes.

________ 9. Every organism has the same number of chromosomes.

________ 10. Body cells have paired chromosomes.

________ 11. Gametes have paired chromosomes.

________ 12. A body cell and a sex cell have the same number of chromosomes.

________ 13. Gametes have half the number of chromosomes of body cells.

________ 14. A human body cell has a total of 23 chromosomes.

________ 15. A human gamete has 23 single chromosomes.

REACHING OUT

Which organism would more closely resemble its parent, one produced by asexual reproduction, or one produced by sexual reproduction? Why? ____________________

____

____

____

What are dominant and recessive traits?

3

dominant [DOM-uh-nunt] **gene:** stronger gene that always shows itself
hybrid [HY-brid]: having two unlike genes
pure: having two like genes
recessive [ri-SES-iv] **gene:** weaker gene that is hidden when the dominant gene is present

LESSON 3 | What are dominant and recessive traits?

Tom has dark hair, just like his parents. Sally's hair is dark too, just like her father. Her mother's hair, however, is blonde.

It is easy to understand why Tom's hair is dark. Both of his parents have dark hair. How about Sally? Why is her hair dark? Why not blonde?

This kind of question was first answered in the mid 1800s by Gregor Mendel, an Austrian monk. Mendel often is called the "Father of Genetics." Mendel observed inherited traits. He wondered why certain traits found in parents show up in their offspring, while other traits do not.

To find the answer, Mendel experimented with pea plants. He observed certain traits such as tallness and shortness, color, and the smoothness of the seed coverings. His experiments led to the Principles of Genetics. These principles hold true for all organisms that reproduce sexually.

One of the principles of genetics is called the Law of Dominance. The Law of Dominance states:

1. An organism receives two genes for each trait, one from each parent.
2. One of the genes may be stronger than the other. The trait of the stronger gene is expressed, or shows up. The gene that shows up is called the **dominant** [DOM-uh-nunt] **gene**. The "hidden" gene is called the **recessive** [ri-SES-iv] **gene** for that trait.

If an offspring receives two of the same genes (either two recessive or two dominant), the offspring will inherit that trait. There is no other possibility.

However, suppose an organism has one dominant gene and one recessive gene for a certain trait. The organism will have the trait of the dominant gene. The recessive gene will be "hidden."

Let's look at Sally again. Sally has genes for dark hair and for light hair. The gene for dark hair is dominant over the gene for light hair. That is why Sally's hair is dark.

It is interesting to note that a trait that is dominant for one kind of organism may be recessive in another organism.

UNDERSTANDING MENDEL'S EXPERIMENTS

What You Need to Know:

Organisms that have two of the same genes for a certain trait are called **pure**.

A pure organism may have two dominant genes or two recessive genes. For example, a pea plant may have two genes for tallness or two genes for shortness. In pea plants, the gene for tallness is dominant.

Organisms that have two unlike genes for a certain trait are called **hybrid** [HY-brid]. A pea plant that has one gene for tallness and one gene for shortness is a hybrid.

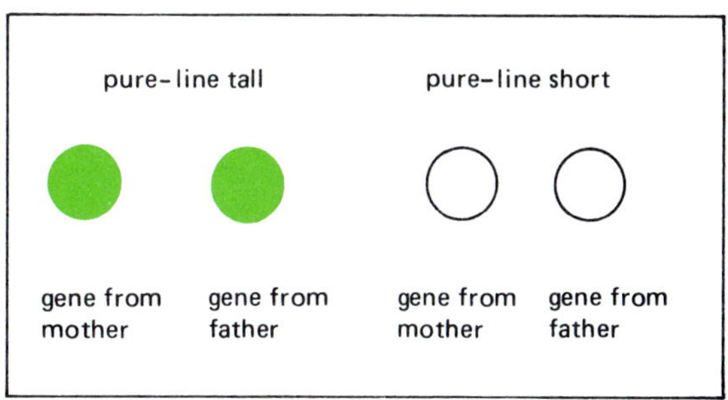

Figure A

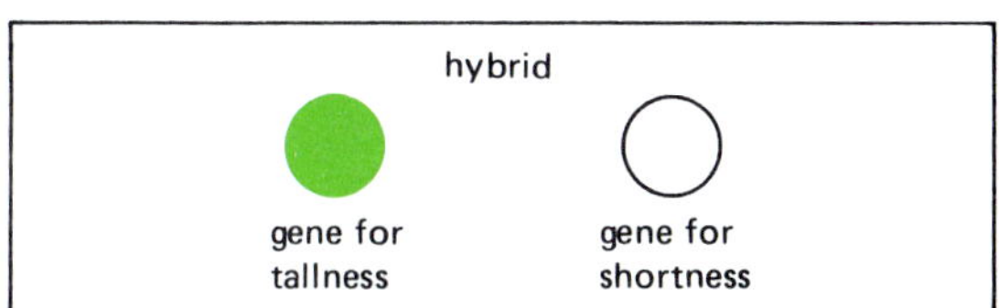

Figure B

No organism has all dominant or all recessive genes.

An organism may be pure in certain traits and hybrid in others. Figures C through F show some of Mendel's experiments with pea plants. Study the figures and answer the questions with each.

Circle the letter of the phrase that completes each sentence best. Fill in the answer blanks for the other sentences.

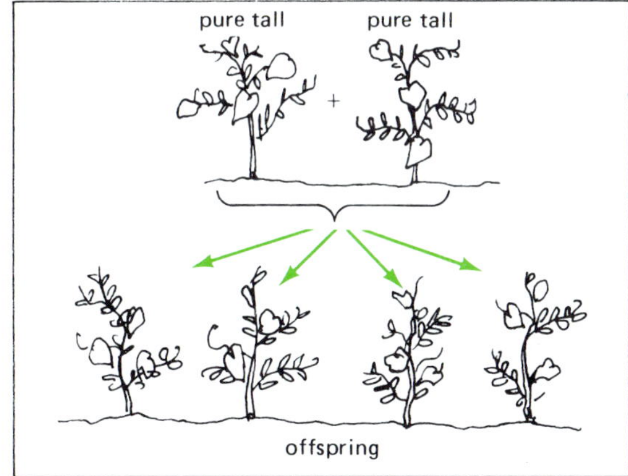

Figure C *Mendel cross-pollinated two pure tall pea plants.*

1. Offspring of pure tall pea plants are

   a) only tall.

   b) only short.

   c) tall and short.

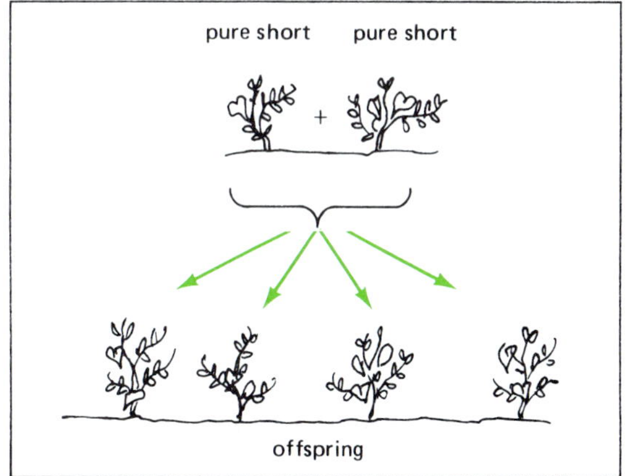

Figure D *Mendal crossed two pure short pea plants.*

2. Offspring of pure short pea plants are

   a) only tall.

   b) only short.

   c) tall and short.

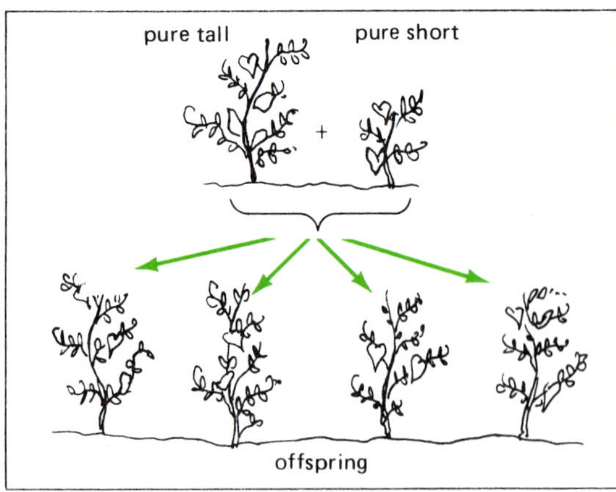

Figure E *Mendel crossed a pure tall with a pure short.*

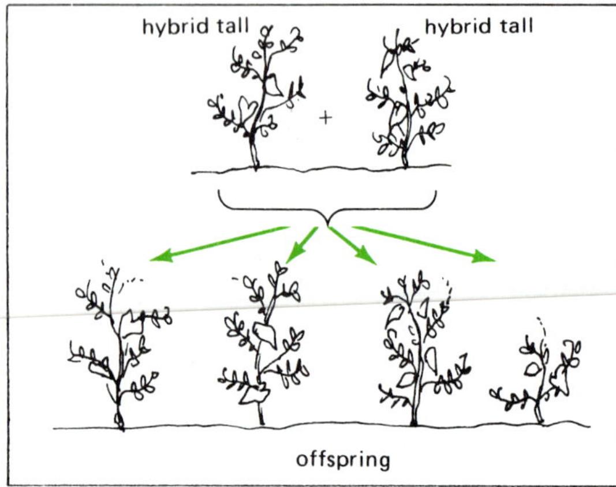

Figure F *Mendel crossed hybrid plants.*

3. Offspring of pure tall pea plants and pure short plants are

a) only tall.

b) only short.

c) short and tall.

4. We see that in pea plants, ____________ (shortness, tallness) is dominant over ____________ (shortness, tallness).

5. The offspring now carry genes of height from both parents. They are

a) genes only for tallness.

b) genes only for shortness.

c) genes for tallness and shortness.

6. The offspring are ____________ (pure, hybrids).

7. Offspring of hybrid-tall pea plants are

a) only tall.

b) only short.

c) short and tall.

8. a) Which is the dominant trait? ____________

b) Does the dominant trait show up in every offspring? ____________

Look at Figure F.

9. a) Which trait is recessive? ____________

b) Is the recessive trait always hidden? ____________

c) How many plants are tall? ____________

d) How many plants are short? ____________

10. Complete the fractions in these sentences:

When you cross hybrids, the dominant trait shows up $\frac{\ }{4}$ of the time.

The recessive trait shows up $\frac{\ }{4}$ of the time.

DOMINANT AND RECESSIVE TRAITS IN HUMANS

How many traits do you recognize in yourself?

Dominant	Recessive
brown eyes	blue eyes
very curly hair	wavy hair
wavy hair	straight hair
freckles	no freckles
nearsightedness	normal eyesight
long eyelashes	short eyelashes
large ears	small ears
dimpled cheeks	no dimples

PREDICTING HUMAN TRAITS

Now use the information from the chart above to fill in the chart below. The first example has been done for you.

	Mother	Father	Offspring	Dominant or Recessive?	Hybrid or Pure?
1.	normal eyes	nearsighted	nearsighted	dominant	hybrid
2.	straight hair	straight hair			
3.	long eyelashes	short eyelashes			
4.	no freckles	no freckles			
5.	no dimples	dimples			
6.	blue eyes	brown eyes			
7.	large ears	large ears			
8.	wavy hair	very curly hair			

Now answer these questions.

9. How many offspring in the chart will be pure recessive for a trait? ____________

10. Why will the recessive genes show up? ______________________________

____

FILL IN THE BLANK

Complete each statement using a term or terms from the list below. Write your answers in the spaces provided. Some words may be used more than once.

hybrid	Gregor Mendel	dominant
recessive	genes	pure
pea plants	are the same	two

1. A pioneer in the study of heredity was ________________ .
2. Mendel studied heredity by experimenting with ________________.
3. Traits are controlled by ________________ .
4. In organisms that reproduce sexually, every trait has genes from ________________ parents.
5. The "stronger" of the two traits which show up in an organism is called the ________________ trait.
6. The "weaker" of the two traits is called the ________________ trait.
7. No organism has all ________________ or all ________________ genes.
8. An organism whose genes for a trait are the same is called ________________ for that trait.
9. An organism whose genes for a trait are not the same, is called ________________ for that trait.
10. An offspring will definitely inherit a trait if both its genes for that trait ________________ .

MATCHING

Match each term in Column A with its description in Column B. Write the correct letter in the space provided.

	Column A	Column B
________	1. dominant trait	a) has mixed genes for a given trait
________	2. recessive trait	b) shows up in offspring
________	3. pure	c) a dominant trait in pea plants
________	4. hybrid	d) has two like genes for a given trait
________	5. tallness	e) may remain "hidden"

How can we predict heredity?

4

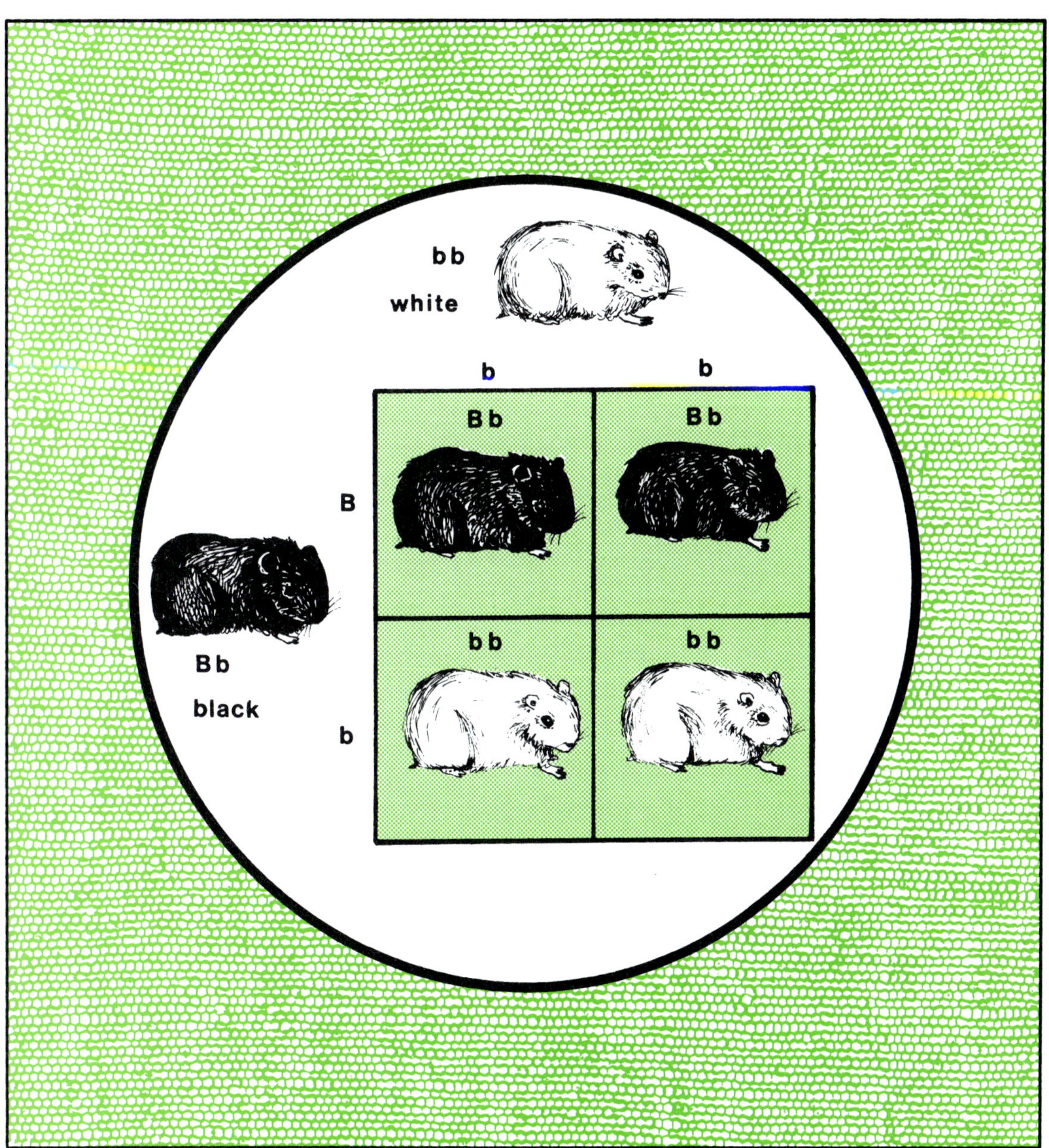

Punnett square: chart used to show possible gene combinations

LESSON 4 | How can we predict heredity?

Meet Mr. and Mrs. Jones:

Tom has two of the same genes for hair color. He is pure for dark hair.

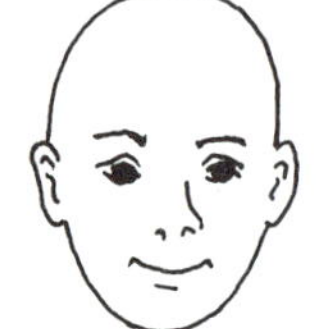

Susan has one dominant gene for dark hair and one recessive gene for blonde hair. She is hybrid.

How can we predict what color hair their children will have? It's easy! We can use a special chart called a **Punnett square**. A Punnett square is a chart used to show possible gene combinations. The steps here show you how to use a Punnett square.

1. Draw a box with four squares in it.

2. Write the gene's from the father across the top of the chart. A dominant gene is always marked with a capital letter "D" stands for dark hair. Both of Tom's genes for hair color are represented by D.

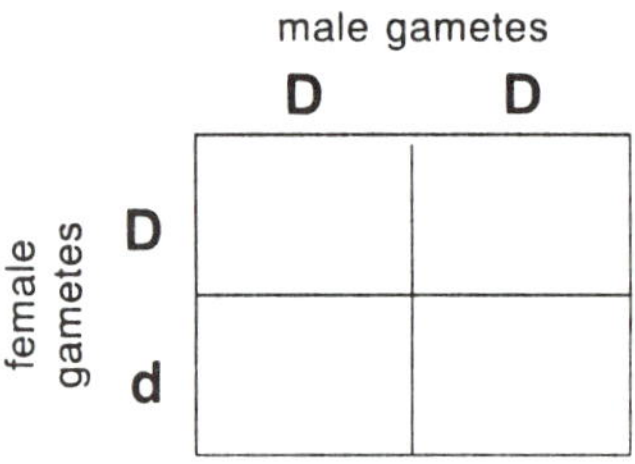

3. Write the genes from the mother down the side of the chart. A recessive gene is always marked with a lower case letter. Susan is hybrid dark for hair color. One gene is marked D. The other gene is the recessive gene for blonde hair. The symbol for this gene is d.

4. Now fill in each box with a gene from the father and a gene from the mother. Each box now shows the different combination of genes that can show up in the offspring.

	D	D
D	DD	DD
d	Dd	Dd

MORE ABOUT PUNNETT SQUARES

Look again at the Punnett square on page 22. What do the letters in the box tell us?

- The possible gene combinations are DD, DD, Dd, and Dd.
- Each combination has a dominant gene for dark hair.
- Therefore all of Tom and Susan's children will have dark hair.

If Tom and Susan have four children, the Punnett square predicts that

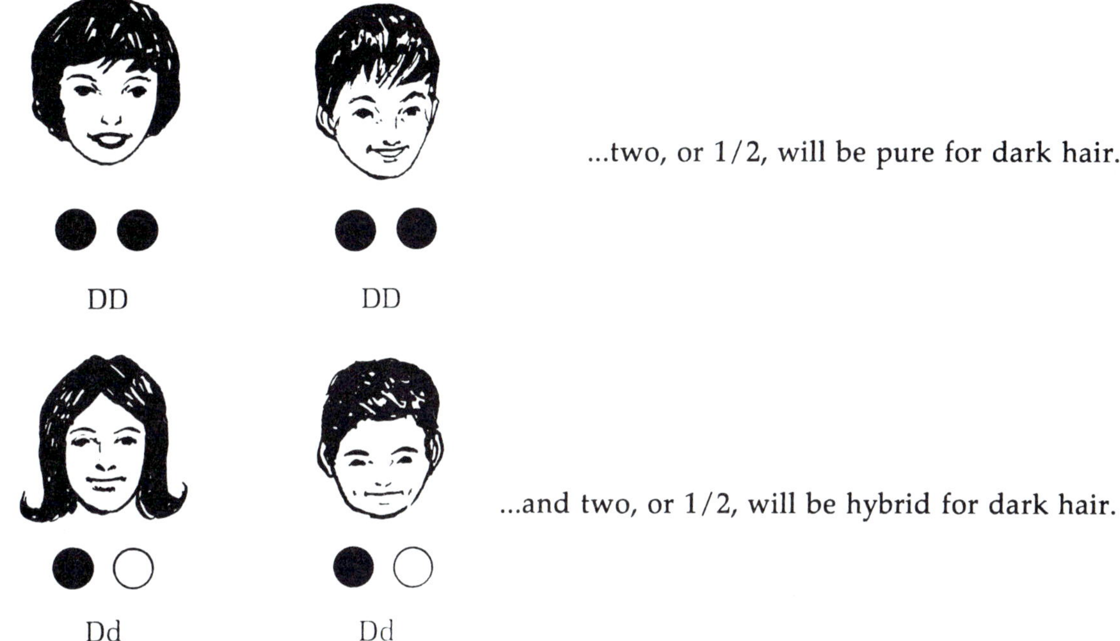

Remember, there are only two possibilities- pure dark and hybrid dark. And you cannot tell by looking at the children which ones are pure and which ones are hybrid for dark hair.

Which gene combinations will turn up in a child? It's a matter of chance.

PREDICTING HEREDITY IN PEA PLANTS

When Mendel did his experiments with pea plants he found that some peas had a smooth covering. Others were wrinkled.

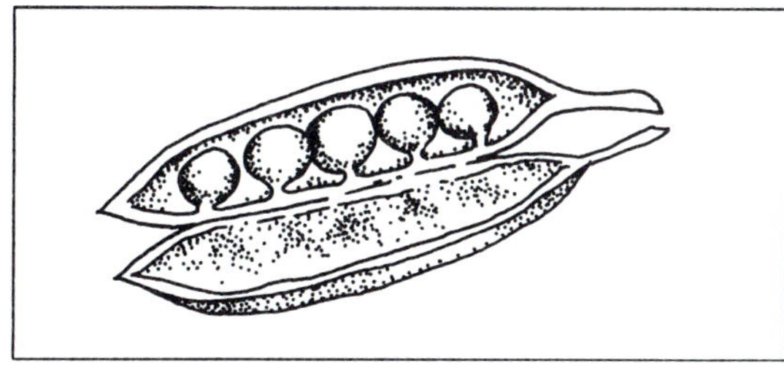

Figure A *Smooth peas are dominant (S).*

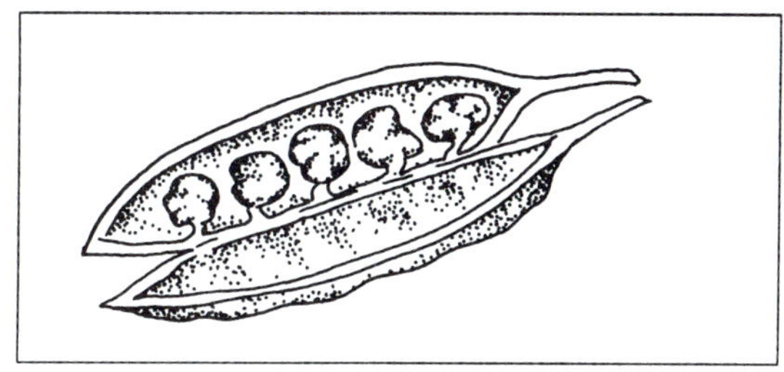

Figure B *Wrinkled peas are recessive (s).*

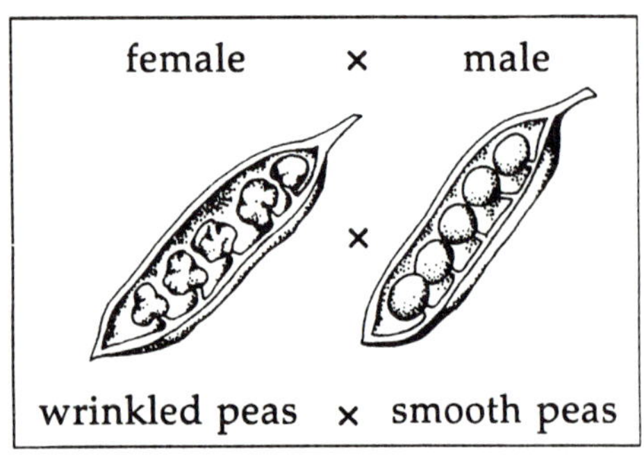

Figure C

Let's see what happens when a pure smooth pea plant is crossed with a pure wrinkled pea plant.

1. The dominant smooth genes come from the

 ______________________ .
 male, female

2. The recessive wrinkled genes come from the

 ______________________ .
 male, female

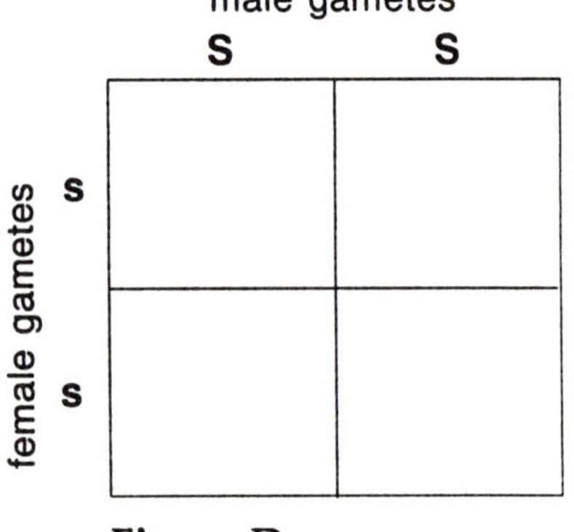

Figure D

3. Now fill in the Punnett square for Figure D.

4. What kind of covering will all the offspring peas have? ______________________
 smooth, wrinkled

5. All the offspring are ______________________ .
 pure, hybrids

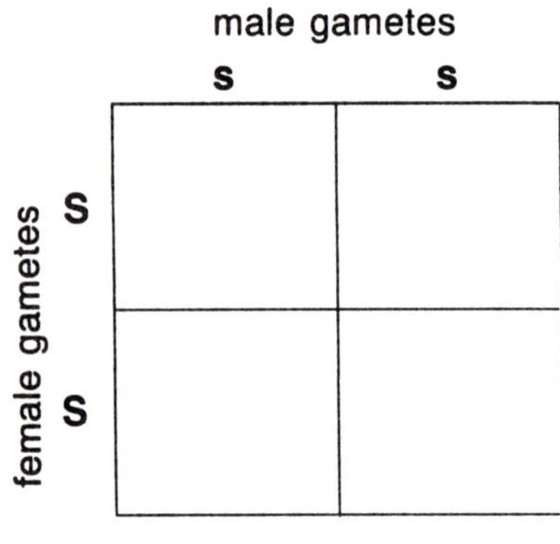

Figure E

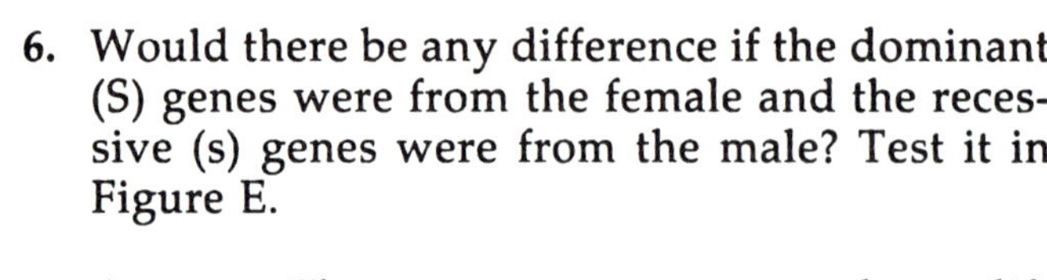

6. Would there be any difference if the dominant (S) genes were from the female and the recessive (s) genes were from the male? Test it in Figure E.

 Answer: There ______________________ be a difference.
 would, would not

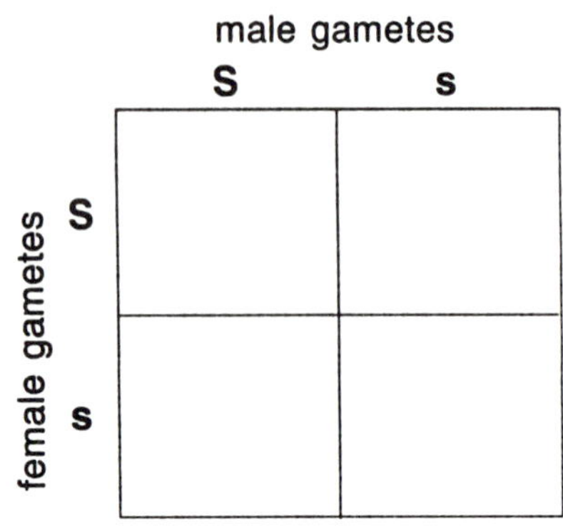

Figure F

Now try a cross between two hybrids, Ss x Ss. Fill in Figure F.

7. How many offspring will be smooth?

 ____

8. How many will be wrinkled? ______________________

9. How many offspring will be pure smooth?

 ____

10. How many will be hybrid smooth? ______________

PREDICTING HUMAN TRAITS

Figure G

Gary and Tina are married. They are planning a family. What will their children look like? Try some more Punnett squares to find out.

Gary is hybrid for curly hair (Cc). Tina is pure for straight hair (cc).

C = dominant curly
c = recessive straight

Gary is hybrid for dark hair (Dd). Tina is pure for blonde hair (dd).

D = dominant dark
d = recessive blonde

Both Gary and Tina are hybrid for brown eyes (Bb).

B = dominant brown
b = recessive blue

Complete the Punnett square for each trait. Then answer the questions.

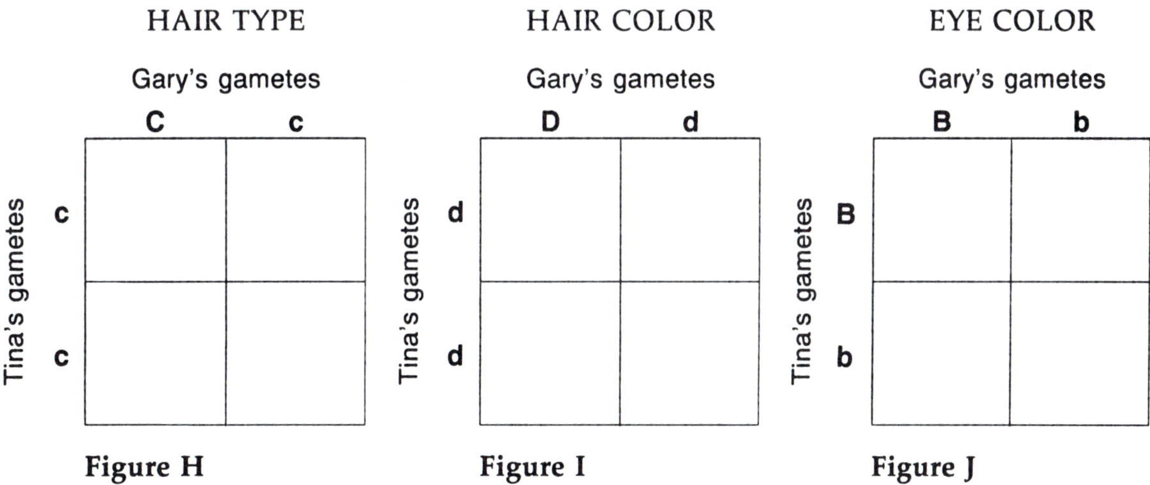

Figure H

Figure I

Figure J

1. How many offspring will have curly hair? ____________________
2. How many offspring will have straight hair? ____________________
3. How many offspring will be pure for curly hair? ____________________
4. How many offspring will be pure for straight hair? ____________________

5. How many will be hybrid for curly hair? ____________

6. How many offspring will have dark hair? ____________

7. How many offspring will have blonde hair? ____________

8. How many offspring will be pure for dark hair? ____________

9. How many will be pure for blonde hair? ____________

10. How many will be hybrid for dark hair? ____________

11. How many offspring will have brown eyes? ____________

12. How many offspring will have blue eyes? ____________

13. How many will be pure for brown eyes? ____________

14. How many will be pure for blue eyes? ____________

15. How many will be hybrid for brown eyes? ____________

MATCHING

Match each term in Column A with its description in Column B. Write the correct letter in the space provided.

	Column A	Column B
________	**1.** Punnett square	**a)** represented by a lower case letter
________	**2.** dominant gene	**b)** male gametes
________	**3.** egg cells	**c)** represented by a capital letter
________	**4.** sperm cells	**d)** female gametes
________	**5.** recessive gene	**e)** used to show gene combinations

What is incomplete dominance?

5

blending: combination of genes in which a mixture of both traits shows
incomplete dominance: blending of traits carried by two or more different genes

LESSON 5 | What is incomplete dominance?

In most games, there is a stronger team and a weaker team. Usually, the stronger team wins. Some games end in ties. This shows that the teams were equally matched.

Heredity is sometimes like this. Most traits have a stronger, dominant gene, and a weaker, recessive gene. The dominant gene usually "wins." The dominant trait shows up in the offspring. The recessive trait stays "hidden."

Not all genes, however, are completely dominant nor completely recessive. The genes of certain traits are equally strong. Neither trait is dominant. We say there is **incomplete dominance.** In cases of incomplete dominance, genes combine and a mixture of both traits shows up. This kind of gene combination is called **blending.**

Three good examples of incomplete dominance are found in the colors of four-o'clock flowers, shorthorn cattle, and Andalusian [an-duh-LEW-zhun] fowl.

Four-o'clock flowers Four-o'clock flowers are usually red or white. Red and white are equally strong traits. Neither color is dominant. When a pure red (RR) crosses with a pure white (WW), the colors blend. The offspring have pink flowers (RW).

Shorthorn cattle In cattle, if one parent is pure red (RR) and the other parent is pure white (WW), the offspring will be pink—a blend of red and white (RW). The "blended" calf is called a roan calf.

Andalusian fowl Some of these chickens have genes for black feathers. Others have genes for white feathers. Neither of these genes is dominant. The offspring of pure black and pure white Andalusians are gray. Gray is a blend of black and white.

Many genes in humans also show incomplete dominance. They include genes for most hair, skin, and eye colors.

UNDERSTANDING BLENDING

Figures A, B, and C show three examples of incomplete dominance.

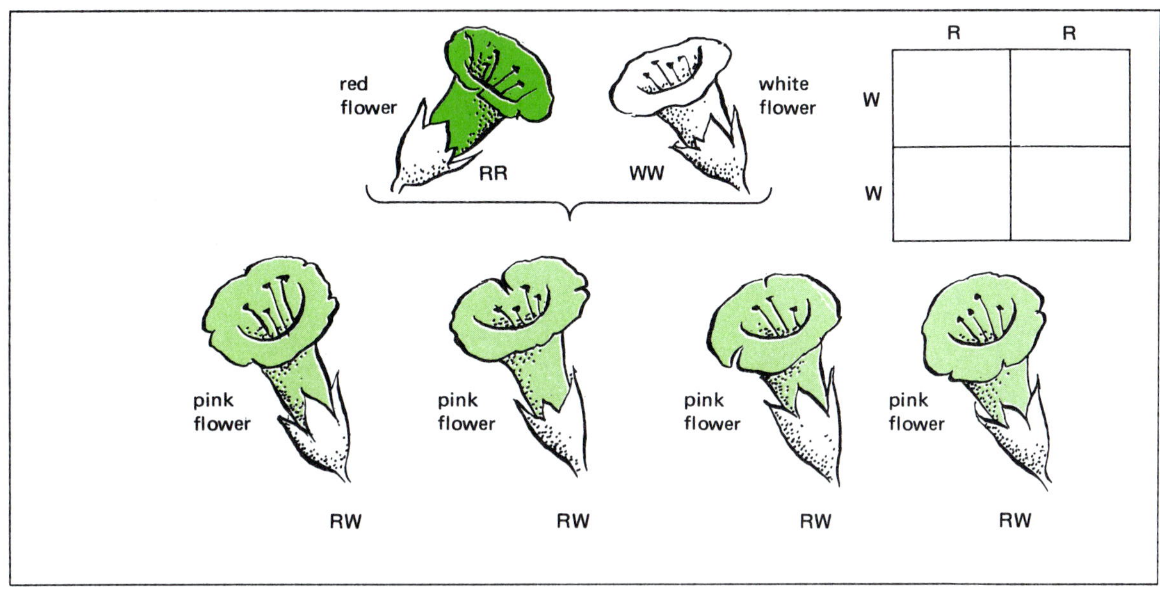

Figure A *The crossing of pure red (RR) and pure white (WW) four-o'clock flowers.*

1. Fill in the Punnett square in Figure A.

_______ 2. The offspring of crossed pure red and pure white four-o'clock flowers are

   a) only red. b) only white.
   c) only pink. d) both red and white.

_______ 3. In four-o'clock flowers,

   a) red is dominant over white. b) white is dominant over red.
   c) neither red nor white is dominant. d) pink is dominant over red.

4. Pink is a blend of which two colors? _______________ and _______________

_______ 5. Blended four-o'clock flowers have

   a) only genes for the color white. b) only genes for the color red.
   c) genes for both red and white. d) only pink genes.

6. Blended four-o'clock flowers are _______________ .
   pure, hybrids

7. Just by looking at the chart in Figure A how can you tell that there is incomplete dominance? _______________________________________

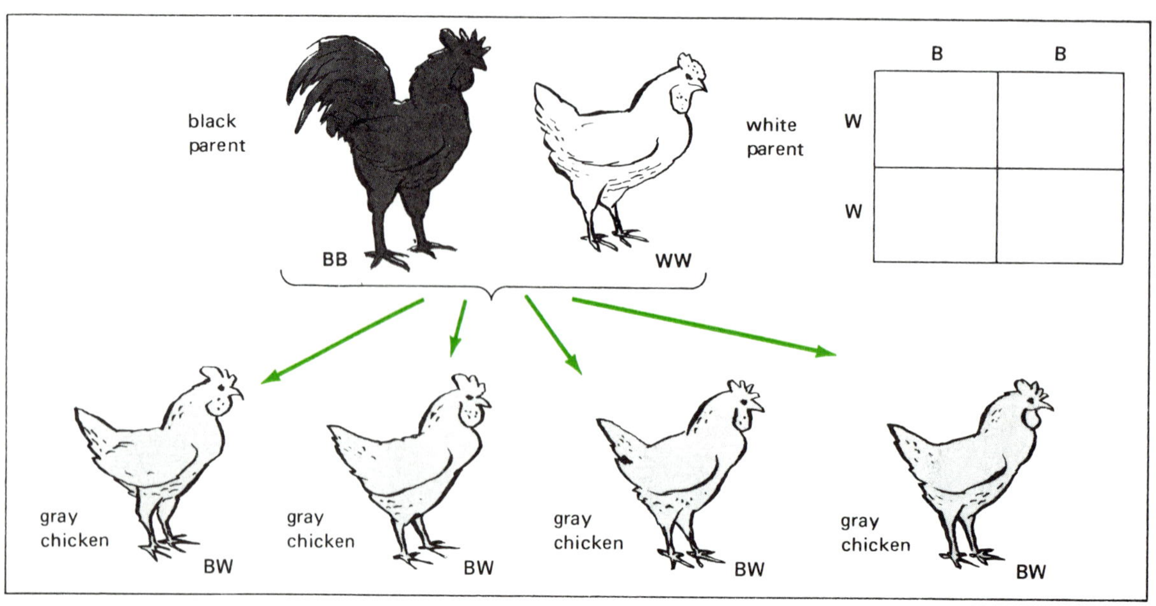

Figure B *The crossing of pure black (BB) and pure white (WW) Andalusian chickens.*

8. Complete the Punnett square in Figure B.

________ **9.** The offspring of crossed pure black and pure white Andalusian chickens are

a) only white. **b)** only black.

c) a blend of black and white. **d)** black and white.

________ **10.** In Andalusian chickens,

a) black is dominant over white. **b)** white is dominant over black.

c) neither black nor white is dominant. **d)** both black and white are dominant.

11. What color are the offspring of black and white chickens?

____

12. Gray is a blend of which two colors? ________________ and

____

________ **13.** Blended Andalusian fowl have

a) only genes for the color black. **b)** only genes for the color white.

c) genes for both black and white. **d)** only grey genes.

14. Blended Andalusian fowl are ________________ .
pure, hybrids

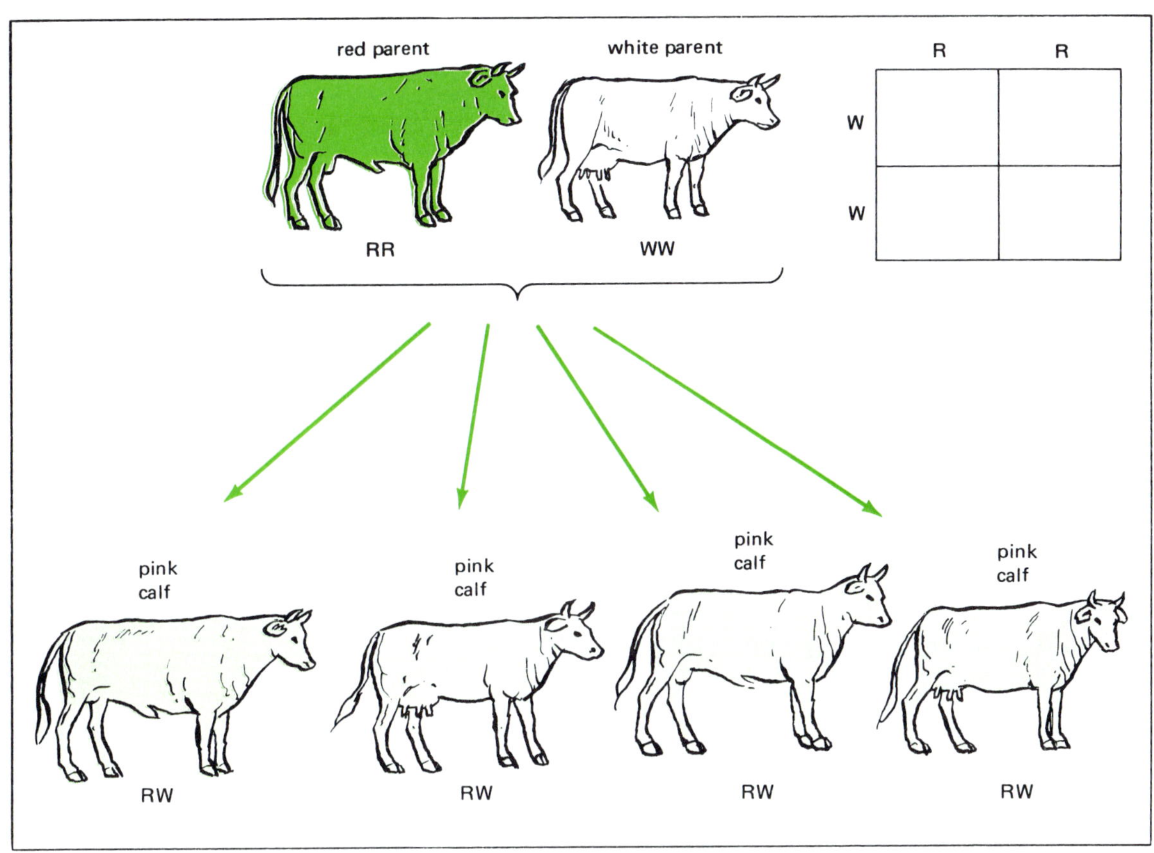

Figure C *The crossing of pure red (RR) and pure white (WW) shorthorn cattle.*

15. Complete the Punnett square in Figure C.

_______ 16. The offspring of crossed pure red and pure white shorthorn cattle are

a) only red.
b) only white.
c) a blend of red and white.
d) red and white.

_______ 17. In shorthorn cattle,

a) red is dominant over white.
b) white is dominant over red.
c) there is incomplete dominance of red and white colors.
d) pink is dominant over white.

18. What are red and white blended cattle called? _______________

_______ 19. Roans have

a) only genes for the color white.
b) only genes for the color red.
c) genes for both white and red.
d) only pink genes.

20. Roans are _______________.
pure, hybrids

FILL IN THE BLANK

Complete each statement using a term or terms from the list below. Write your answers in the spaces provided. Some words may be used more than once.

blending	dominant	incomplete dominance
roan calf	red	skin
recessive	eye	pure
white	pink four-o'clock flower	hybrid
		strong

1. A "hidden trait" is called a ________________ trait.
2. Not all genes are completely recessive nor completely ________________ . Some are equally ________________.
3. An individual that has only dominant or recessive genes for a trait is ________________ for that trait.
4. An individual that has both dominant and recessive genes for a trait is ________________ for that trait.
5. A condition where the genes for a given trait are equally strong is called ________________________ .
6. A combination of genes in which a mixture of both traits shows up is called ________________ .
7. Two examples of offspring of incomplete dominance are ________________ and the ________________________ .
8. In four-o'clock flowers and roan cattle, neither the color ________________ nor the color ________________ is dominant.
9. Incomplete dominance produces offspring with ________________ genes for the given trait.
10. Examples of incomplete dominance in humans are found in ________________ and ________________ color.

MATCHING

Match each term in Column A with its description in Column B. Write the correct letter in the space provided.

	Column A	Column B
________	**1.** RR	**a)** recessive pure
________	**2.** Rr	**b)** control heredity
________	**3.** rr	**c)** blends traits
________	**4.** incomplete dominance	**d)** dominant pure
________	**5.** genes	**e)** hybrid

Complete the Punnet square for feather color in chickens.

B = black feathers

W = white feathers

BW = gray feathers

	W	**W**
B		
B		

1. Are the parents in this cross pure or hybrids? ________________

2. What color are the parents? ________________

3. Will all of the offspring produced by this cross be hybrids? ________________

4. What colors will the offspring be? ________________

5. Why is neither gene in this cross represented by a lower case letter? ________________

____

WORD SCRAMBLE

Below are several scrambled words you have used in this Lesson. Unscramble the words and write your answers in the spaces provided.

1. TOMANDIN ________________

2. SEERVICES ________________

3. DLEBN ________________

4. RATTI ________________

5. DHSYIRB ________________

SCIENCE *EXTRA*

Spooky Siblings

When Jerry Levey and Mark Newman saw each other for the first time, they were stunned. But they had no trouble recognizing each other, for they were identical twins who had grown up apart. They were reunited as adults by accident. During one of their first conversations, they found out how much they had in common. "We kept making the same remarks at the same time and using the same gestures. It was spooky," said Jerry. Identical twins reared apart are being studied by scientists to learn how genes affect personality.

How do scientists study the genetics of personality? A research team at the University of Minnesota has studied hundreds of pairs of identical twins, some raised together, some apart. Scientists also study fraternal twins reared together to compare the effect of common upbringing on siblings.

The scientists, led by Dr. Thomas Bouchard, measure 11 personality traits, including things such as impulsiveness and reaction to stress. So far, their analysis shows that identical twins reared apart and together are very much alike in personality. Identical twins reared together are quite different from fraternal twins reared together in overall heritability of personality traits.

It is important to remember that identical twins are genetic copies of each other. Identical twins happen when the zygote, splits into two before any cell division takes place. Thus the twins develop from the same egg and the same sperm. Fraternal twins, on the other hand, develop from two different eggs. On average, fraternal twins share about half of their genes.

Scientists still have not explained how genes determine personality. Nor have they identified specific genes for personality traits. These are questions for future scientists to answer. But the study does explain a lot of things about the twins reared apart. Said Mark Newman, "I used to feel something was missing. Now it's back in place."

How is sex determined? 6

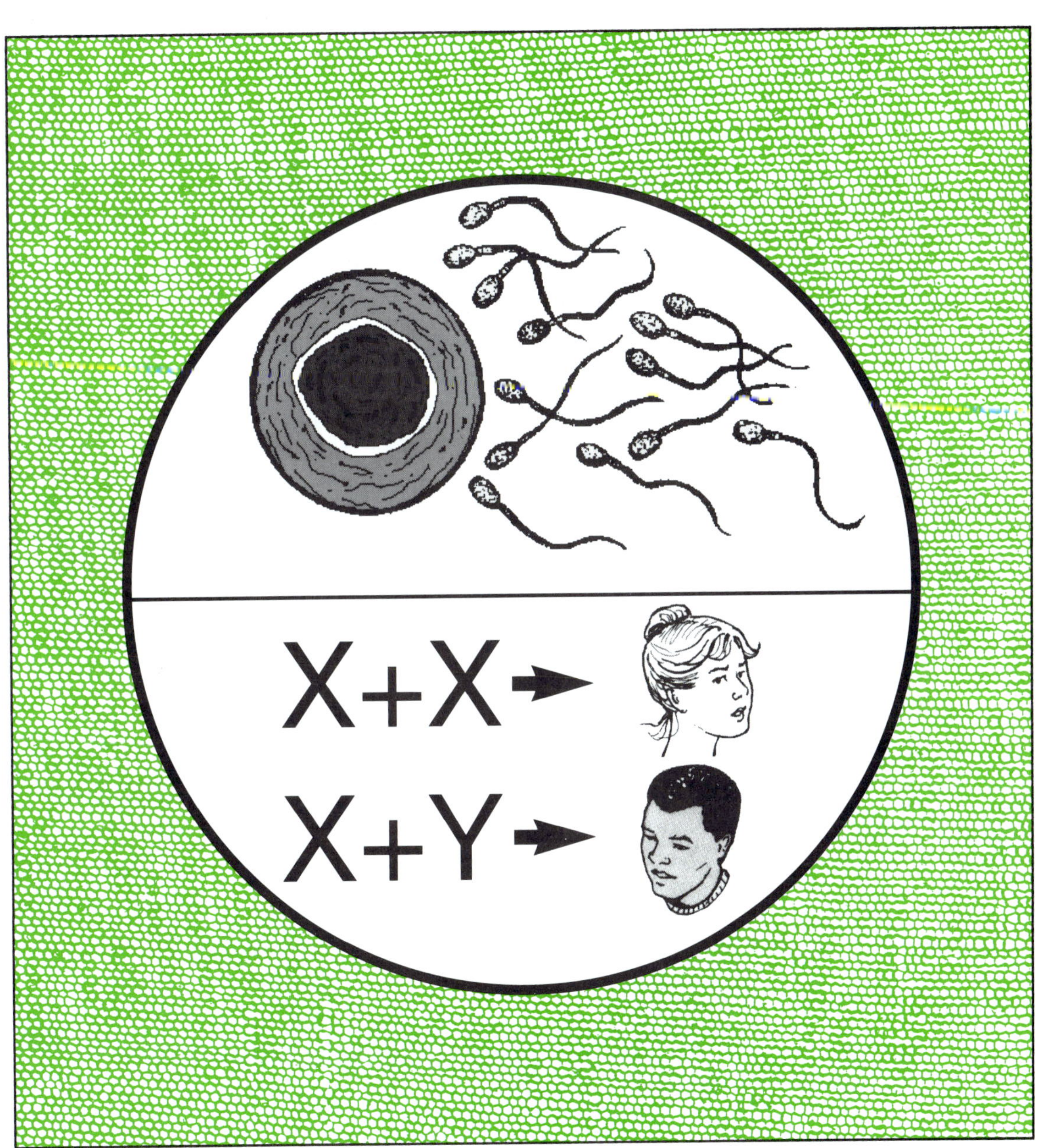

sex chromosomes: X and Y chromosomes

LESSON 6 | How is sex determined?

Will the baby be a boy or a girl? Every expectant parent asks this question. Well, the possibilities are even—50 percent for a boy, 50 percent for a girl. It depends entirely upon chance.

A single family may have more girls than boys, or more boys than girls. The population on the whole is just about even—half male and half female. Let us find out why.

Look at the 23 pairs of human chromosomes below.

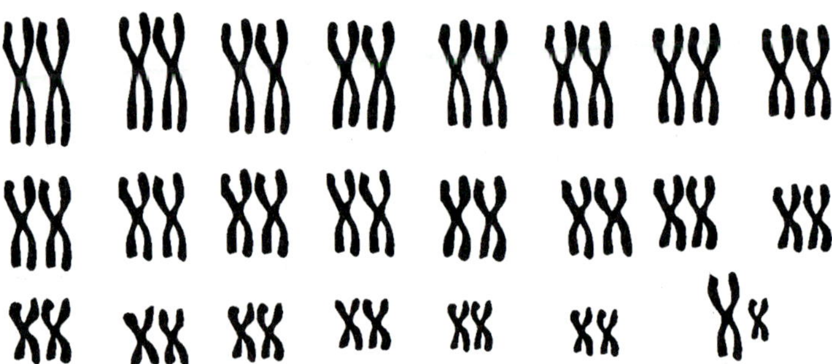

Chromosomes from a body cell of a human male

Notice that each chromosome in a pair is the same size and shape—except for the last pair. In a male, the chromosomes in the last pair are different. The larger is called the X chromosome. The smaller is the Y chromosome. X and Y chromosomes are the **sex chromosomes.** They determine the sex of most organisms.

- A male cell has one X chromosome and one Y chromosome (XY).
- A female cell has two X chromosomes (XX).

What determines the sex of an offspring? The next page tells the story. We will use the fruit fly as an example.

HOW MALE GAMETES DETERMINE SEX

A fruit fly body cell has eight chromosomes (four pairs). Two of these (one pair) are sex chromosomes. Special body cells produce gametes, or sex cells, by the process of meiosis. Meiosis is a special kind of cell division.

FRUIT FLY

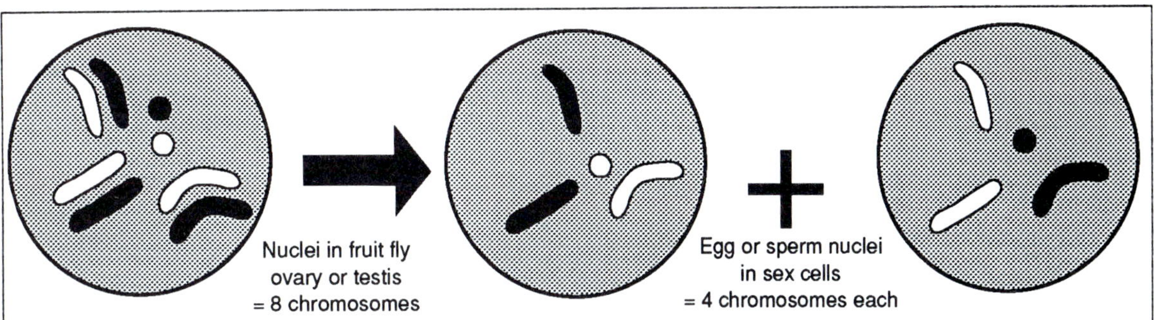

Figure A

In a male, meiosis produces four sperm cells from one body cell. During meiosis, each sperm cell receives only one sex chromosome from a pair. In a female, meiosis produces one usable egg cell and three unusable cells from one body cell. During meiosis, each egg cell receives one sex chromosome from a pair.

HOW EGG AND SPERM CELLS ARE PRODUCED IN FRUIT FLIES

Gamete chromosomes are not paired. They are single chromosomes. A gamete, then, has half the number of chromosomes of a body cell. Count them.

Look at the sex chromosome of each gamete.

- An egg has an X chromosome only.

- A sperm may have an X or a Y chromosome; 50 percent have an X chromosome; 50 percent have a Y chromosome.

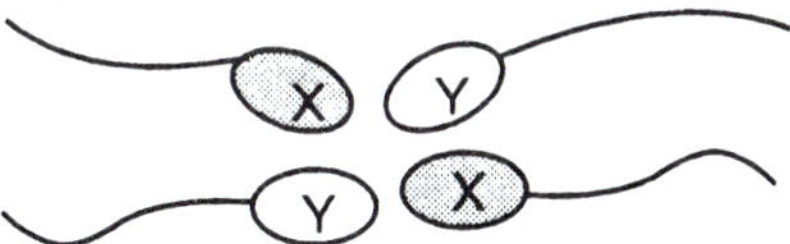

Now here is where chance comes in.

- If an X sperm fertilizes an egg (X + X), the offspring will be a female (XX).

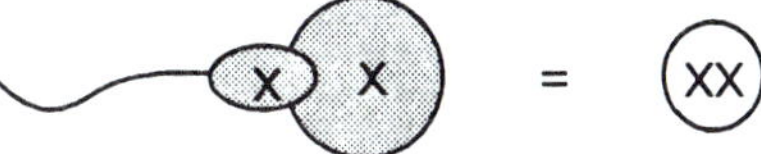

- If a Y sperm fertilizes an egg (Y + X), the offspring will be a male (XY).

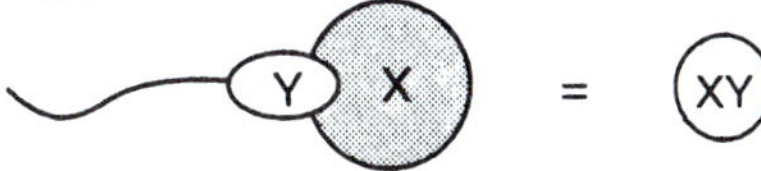

As a result, offspring inherit their sex from their father. Since half of sperm carry the X chromosome and half carry the Y chromosome, over a large number of births, half will be female and half will be male.

Male or female? The chances are 50-50. See for yourself in Figure B.

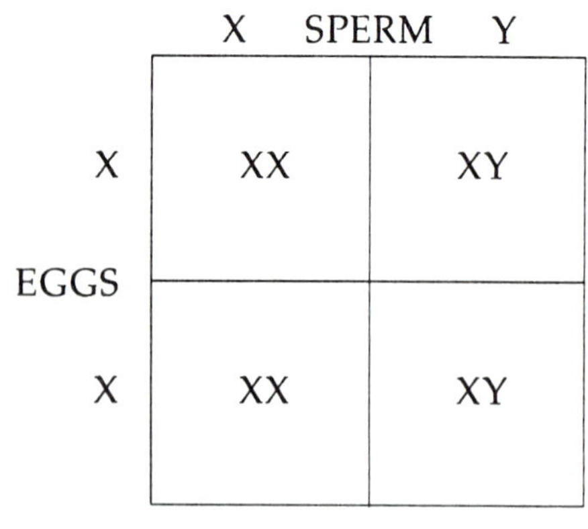

		SPERM	
		X	Y
EGGS	X	XX	XY
	X	XX	XY

Figure B

XX = female — 50 percent
XY = male — 50 percent

Sperm have tails and are able to swim. Millions of sperm may swim toward the same egg, but only one can fertilize it.

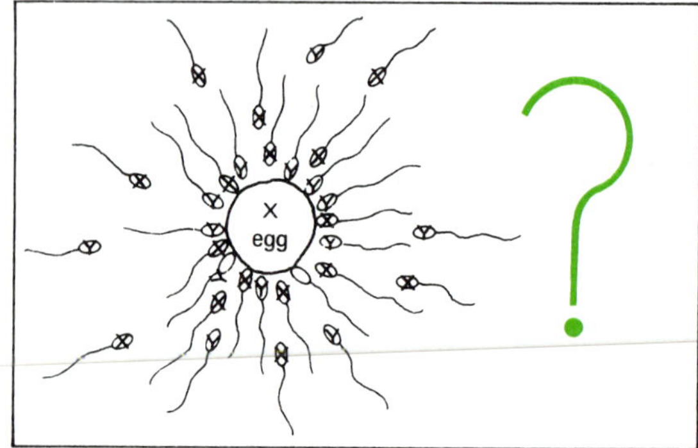

Figure C

Will it be an X sperm or a Y sperm? It depends upon chance!

1. If an X sperm fertilizes the egg, the offspring will be a ______________ (male, female).

2. If a Y sperm fertilizes the egg, the offspring will be a ______________ (male, female).

Study the human chromosomes shown. Then, in the space provided, identify whether a child with these chromosomes is a male child or a female child.

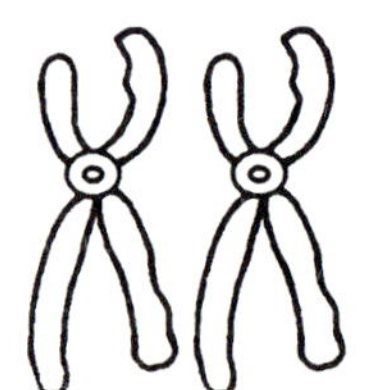

Figure D

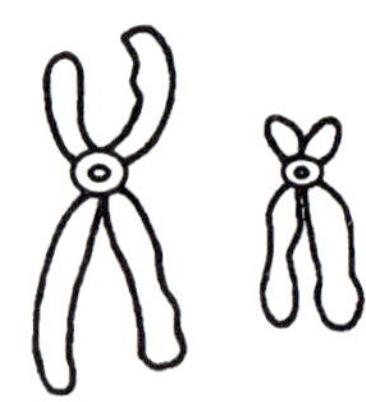

Figure E

3.  ______________

4. ______________

5. Explain your answers. ______________________________

____

____

FILL IN THE BLANK

Complete each statement using a term or terms from the list below. Write your answers in the spaces provided. Some words may be used more than once.

chance	X	gametes
female	half	50-50
Y	male	

1. There are two kinds of sex chromosomes. They are called ______________ and ______________ .
2. A female body cell has only ______________ sex chromosomes.
3. A male body cell has both ______________ and ______________ sex chromosomes.
4. Meiosis produces ______________ .
5. A gamete has ______________ the number of chromosomes found in a body cell.
6. Eggs have only ______________ sex chromosomes.
7. Sperm have either ______________ or ______________ sex chromosomes.
8. Which will fertilize an egg, an X sperm or a Y sperm? It depends entirely upon ______________ . The odds are ______________ .
9. The fertilization of an egg by an X sperm produces a ______________ offspring.
10. The fertilization of an egg by a Y sperm produces a ______________ offspring.

MATCHING

Match each term in Column A with its description in Column B. Write the correct letter in the space provided.

	Column A	Column B
________	**1.** X and Y chromosomes	**a)** XY
________	**2.** male	**b)** sex chromosomes
________	**3.** meiosis	**c)** XX
________	**4.** sperm	**d)** special cell division
________	**5.** female	**e)** male gamete

TRUE OR FALSE

In the space provided, write "true" if the sentence is true. Write "false" if the sentence is false.

________ 1. A body cell has paired chromosomes.

________ 2. A gamete has paired chromosomes.

________ 3. An egg has only a Y sex chromosome.

________ 4. A sperm can have either an X or a Y sex chromosome.

________ 5. An X chromosome looks the same as a Y chromosome.

________ 6. Many sperm fertilize one egg.

________ 7. Fertilization by an X sperm produces a female.

________ 8. Fertilization by a Y sperm produces a male.

________ 9. Humans have 23 pairs of chromosomes.

________ 10. About the same number of male and female organisms are born.

FLIP A COIN

Flip a coin 100 times. Count how many times it lands on heads, and how many times it lands on tails.

1. How many times did it land on heads? ________________

2. How many times did it land on tails? ________________

3. Is it about 50-50? ________________

4. Is flipping a coin a chance event? ________________

5. What other chance event did you learn about in this lesson? ________________

____

____

How does the environment affect traits?

7

LESSON 7 | How does the environment affect traits?

What makes you the way you are? Genes? Of course! Genes control many of your traits. Genes do not work alone. The environment also affects the traits of living things.

The environment is made up of all the living and nonliving things that surround an organism. Air, water, temperature, and food are all parts of the environment. The right combination of these things is needed for an organism to develop properly. When the environment is not right for an organism, certain traits may not develop at all.

Green plants, for example, need an environment of proper sunlight, temperature, water, and minerals to grow well. In a poor environment, they grow small, weak, and pale. The size of a plant is a trait. The gene for this trait is not affected by the environment, but the development of the trait is.

Suppose a person has the genes for growing tall. A poor diet may prevent full growth.

Diet is just one part of your environment. There are many other things that make up your environment. Can you name some that have not been listed.

We cannot change our genes. But, we can change some parts of the environment in which we live. Eating, resting, and exercising properly help the traits we are born with develop to their fullest.

WHAT DO THE PICTURES SHOW?

Traits need a proper environment to develop properly.

Figure A

Figure B

1. In which figure do you see a plant that grew in a good environment? ___________
2. How can you tell? ____

   ____
3. In which figure do you see a plant that grew in a poor environment? ___________
4. How can you tell? ____

   ____

These two rats were born in the same litter. One ate a poor diet; the other ate a diet rich in nutrients.

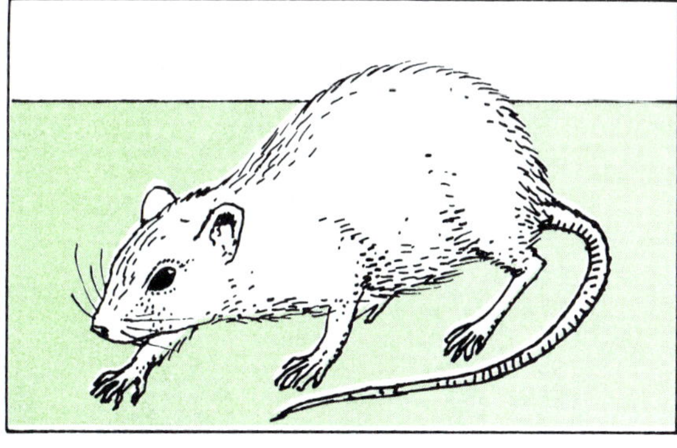

Figure C

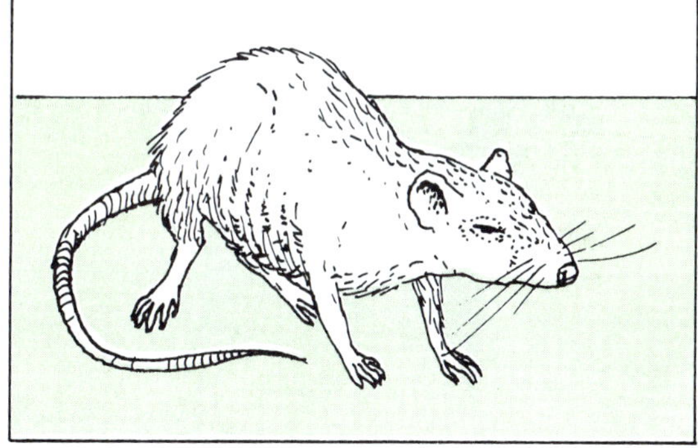

Figure D

5. Is diet part of a living thing's environment? ___________________
6. Which figure shows the rat that ate a poor diet? ___________________
7. How do you know? ____
8. Which figure shows the rat that ate a good diet? ___________________

9. How do you know? ______________________________

____

10. In your own words, what does environment mean? ______________________________

____

____

ARE ALL TRAITS INHERITED?

Many traits are not inherited. These traits are called acquired traits.

Here are some examples of acquired traits.

Figure E *Some people develop strong muscles by exercising.*

Figure F *Some people learn to speak many languages.*

Figure G *The tails of some dogs are cut off at birth.*

Figure H *Trees near the tops of mountains do not grow tall partly because of low temperatures.*

WHAT DO YOU THINK?

Can acquired traits be passed on to an offspring? In other words, can acquired traits be inherited? Answer this question yourself.

1. If parents develop strong muscles by exercising, will their children inherit strong muscles? ________________ (yes, no)
2. Suppose you have learned to speak a new language, will your children be born with this ability? ________________ (yes, no)
3. Suppose the dog in Figure G has puppies. Will they be born without tails? ______
4. Conclusion: Acquired traits ________________ (are, are not) inherited.
5. What kind of traits do you think are inherited? ____________________________

FILL IN THE BLANK

Complete each statement using a term or terms from the list below. Write your answers in the spaces provided. Some words may be used more than once.

living	traits	inherited
acquired	nonliving	environment
genes	good	

1. The characteristics of an individual are called ________________ .
2. Inherited traits are passed on to offspring by ________________ .
3. Some traits develop properly only in a proper ________________ .
4. The environment includes all the ________________ and ________________ things surrounding an organism.
5. Traits that are not inherited are called ________________ traits.
6. Acquired traits are not ________________ .
7. Traits develop best in a ________________ environment.
8. We cannot change our ________________ .
9. A trait that is not carried by genes is an ________________ trait.
10. Air, water, food, and temperature are all parts of the ________________ .

MATCHING

Match each term in Column A with its description in Column B. Write the correct letter in the space provided.

	Column A	Column B
________	1. acquired traits	a) not inherited
________	2. environment	b) genes
________	3. proper environment	c) everything surrounding an individual
________	4. carriers of inherited traits	d) best for developing traits
________	5. trait	e) any characteristic of a living thing

TRUE OR FALSE

In the space provided, write "true" if the sentence is true. Write "false" if the sentence is false.

________ 1. Every trait is carried by genes.

________ 2. Every trait is inherited.

________ 3. A trait that is not carried by genes is an acquired trait.

________ 4. Offspring inherit the acquired traits of their parents.

________ 5. Environment affects how traits develop.

________ 6. Traits develop best in a poor environment.

________ 7. We can control part of our environment.

________ 8. You can inherit genes for strong muscles.

________ 9. Exercise can make strong muscles even stronger.

________ 10. Extra-strong muscles developed by exercise can be inherited.

What are some methods of plant and animal breeding?

8

controlled breeding: mating organisms to produce offspring with certain traits
hybridization [hy-brid-ih-ZAY-shun]: mating two different kinds of organisms
inbreeding: mating closely related organisms
mass selection: crossing organisms with desirable traits

LESSON 8 What are some methods of plant and animal breeding?

You have probably eaten corn on the cob. Have you ever eaten an ear of corn that is only as long as your thumb? Perhaps you have, but we usually think of corn as a large-sized vegetable.

Tiny ears of corn were all that existed thousands of years ago. However, the Indians in South and Central America changed that. They noticed that in nature some ears of corn were larger than others. So they crossed the plants with the largest ears. They found that the offspring were likely to have large ears, too. For many years the Indians selected only the seeds from the largest ears to reproduce. As a result, the size of corn ears greatly increased. A new variety of plant had developed.

The mating of animals and plants to produce certain desirable traits is called **controlled breeding**. People bred animals and plants long before they knew about chromosomes and genes. Now we know much more about genetics. We use this information to produce organisms that are useful to people.

Breeding helps supply the hungry world with food. Plants can be bred to produce larger and better crops. Animals can be bred to produce more and better meat, milk, and wool.

Breeding also serves special needs. For example, breeding has given us giant flowers with unusual colors. We now also have faster racehorses. Even dogs are bred for special jobs such as protection and to help guide the blind.

Sometimes scientists breed plants and animals in laboratories. There, chromosomes can be studied under powerful microscopes. These experiments have led to many discoveries. As a result of these discoveries, scientists can now detect and control certain diseases. Our knowledge of how traits are passed on has certainly increased since Mendel's time.

CONTROLLED BREEDING

Figures A through D show methods of controlled breeding. Study each figure and answer the questions.

Figure A *Mass selection*

To grow corn with large ears, the Indians of South and Central America used a method of controlled breeding. They crossed plants with good traits and then collected and planted the seeds for many plant generations.

Today we call this method **mass selection.**

1. What is the purpose of mass selection?

____

____

Figure B *Inbreeding*

Another breeding method is **inbreeding.** Inbreeding is the mating of closely related organisms.

Inbreeding is used to keep certain kinds of animals pure. For example, thoroughbred racehorses are bred for speed.

2. Inbreeding produces organisms with

very _______________ genes.
similar, different

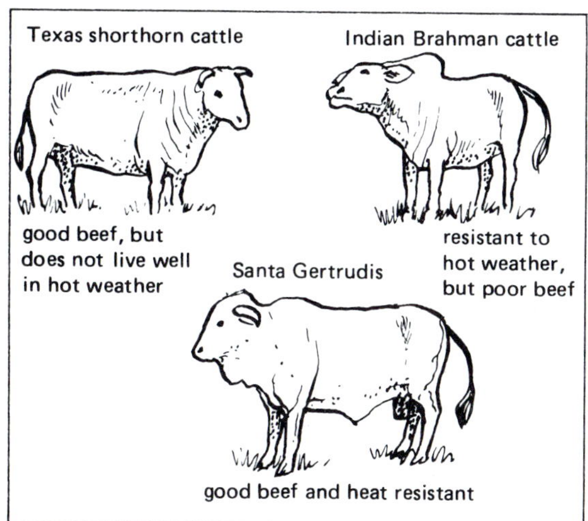

Figure C *Cross-breeding*

Sometimes related, but different, breeds of animals or plants are mated. This combines desired traits.

3. What kind of climate do you think the Indian Brahman came from?

____

4. a) If you were a Texas cattle rancher, which breed would you want?

____

b) Why? _______________________________

____

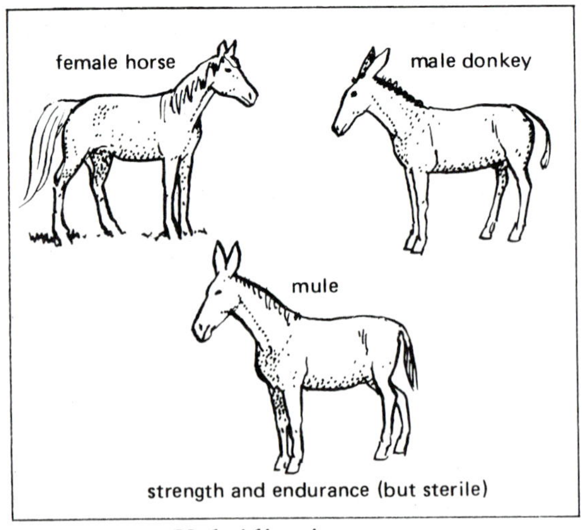

Figure D *Hybridization*

Sometimes two different species of plants or animals are mated. This is called **hybridization** [hy-brid-ih-ZAY-shun]. This can also combine desirable traits. However, the offspring are usually sterile. They are unable to reproduce.

5. Are mules able to reproduce?

____

Figure E

The controlled breeding of animals and plants helps increase food production.

6. Why is greater food production important to the world's population?

____

____

____

____

Breeding improves quality and gives us plants and animals with special traits.

Figure F

7. Do you think that all the food you eat is the same as the food people ate a hundred years ago? ______________

PLANT AND ANIMAL BREEDING

Decide which of the statements refers to mass selection (M), inbreeding (I), or hybridization (H). In the spaces provided, write the correct letter for each statement.

_______ 1. Crossing of closely related organisms

_______ 2. Planting seeds that show desired traits

_______ 3. Organisms used are genetically different

_______ 4. Crossing of plants with desired traits

_______ 5. Self-pollination in plants

_______ 6. Offspring in a male lion and female tiger

_______ 7. Crossing wheat and rye plants.

_______ 8. New varieties of wheat were bred to produce more protein

_______ 9. Have genes very similar to their parents

_______ 10. Purebred dog

NOW TRY THESE

Read the examples. Complete the table by writing the letters of the examples in the correct columns.

Examples

a. Farmer wants sweet corn seeds that will produce tall plants with a high yield.

b. Seed producer wants to develop corn that will resist drought.

c. Dog breeder wants purebred dogs.

d. Offspring of a male donkey and a female horse.

e. Florist wants roses with large petals.

Controlled Breeding

	Method	Example
1.	Mass selection	
2.	Inbreeding	
3.	Hybridization	

TRUE OR FALSE

In the space provided, write "true" if the sentence is true. Write "false" if the sentence is false.

________ 1. Every farm acre grows the same size crop.

________ 2. Every cow gives the same amount of milk.

________ 3. Breeding is controlled reproduction.

________ 4. Breeding helps increase our food supply.

________ 5. In breeding, the best animals are selected for reproduction.

________ 6. Breeding passes on desirable traits.

________ 7. All wheat plants are the same.

________ 8. Breeding can develop animals that are more resistant to heat.

________ 9. Mules are sterile.

________ 10. Inbreeding produces organisms with very different genes.

MATCHING

Match each term in Column A with its description in Column B. Write the correct letter in the space provided.

	Column A	Column B
________	1. controlled breeding	a) mating only closely related organisms
________	2. inbreeding	b) mating related, but different breeds
________	3. mass selection	c) methods used to produce organisms with desirable traits
________	4. cross-breeding	d) mating different species of animals
________	5. hybridization	e) used to develop new plant varieties

REACHING OUT

Inbreeding produces organisms that are very similar genetically. They have few genetic differences. Why do you think this is a problem to a species? ________________

____

____

What is genetic engineering?

9

cloning: production of organisms with identical genes

gene splicing [SPLYS-ing]: moving a section of DNA from the genes of one organism to the genes of another organism

genetic engineering [juh-NET-ik en-juh-NEER-ing]: methods used to produce new forms of DNA

LESSON 9 | What is genetic engineering?

Have you ever seen a supermouse? Supermouse is not a character in a cartoon. It is the nickname given to a mouse produced by researchers. Supermouse is twice the size of a normal mouse. It is the result of a new technology called **genetic engineering** [juh-NET-ik en-juh-NEER-ing]. In genetic engineering, scientists work with individual genes.

In lesson 2, you learned that genes are made up of a complex substance called DNA. Genetic engineering is a process by which new forms of DNA are made.

One method of genetic engineering is called **gene splicing** [SPLYS-ing]. Gene splicing is the process by which pieces of DNA, from the genes of one organism are transferred to another organism.

Gene splicing takes place in three steps. Look at Figures A through D on the next page as you read about these steps.

1. A DNA chain is opened up.
2. New genes from another organism are added, or spliced, into the DNA.
3. The DNA chain is closed.

Once the genes are transferred, they become part of the receiving organism's genes. As a result, the trait carried by the genes is passed on to future generations.

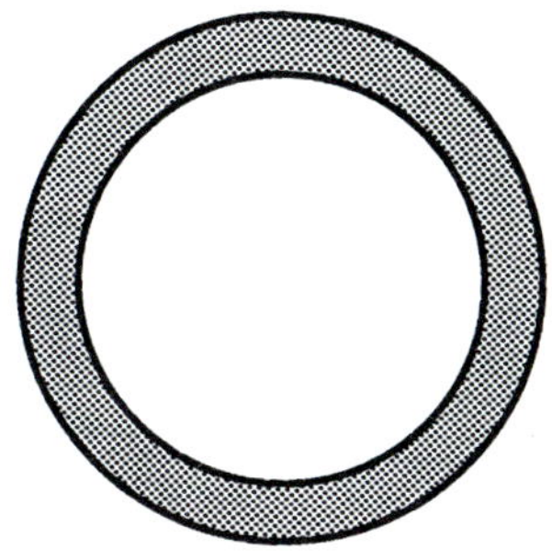

A ring of DNA.

Figure A

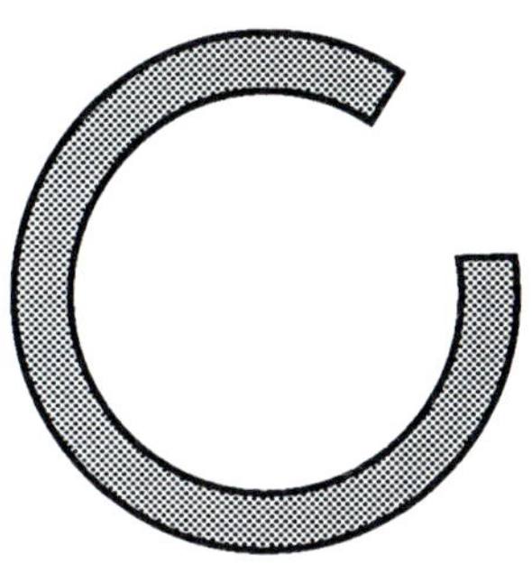

The DNA chain is opened up.

Figure B

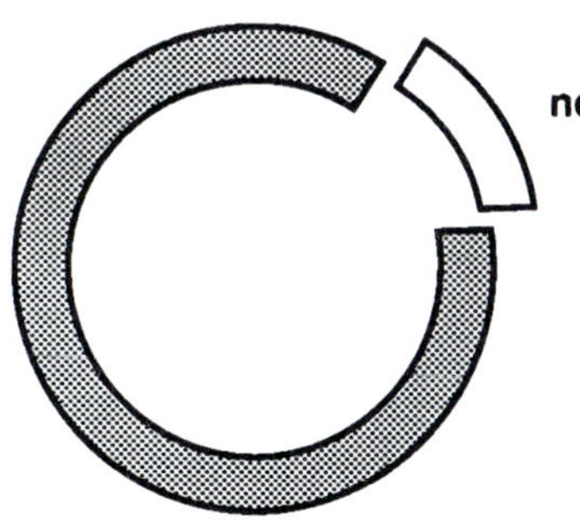

A new strand of DNA, or gene, is added into the ring of DNA.

Figure C

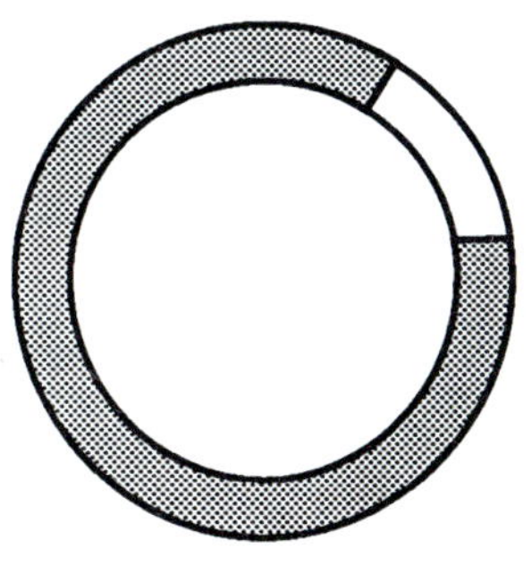

The DNA chain is closed.

Figure D

BENEFITS OF GENETIC ENGINEERING

Through genetic engineering, scientists have been able to splice human genes into the DNA of bacteria. The bacteria can then produce substances that otherwise could only be made by the human body. Here are some substances produced by bacteria through genetic engineering.

INSULIN [IN-suh-lin] Insulin is needed by people with diabetes [dy-uh-BEET-is]. Insulin controls the level of sugar in your blood.

HUMAN GROWTH HORMONE Human growth hormone controls growth. It is given to children who do not make enough of their own growth hormone. This helps the children grow properly.

INTERFERON [in-tur-FEER-ahn] Interferon helps your body fight disease. It is used by scientists in cancer research.

Scientists also hope that someday genetic engineering can be used to correct some genetic disorders. They may be able to add normal genes to cells that have abnormal genes or are missing a gene completely.

TRUE OR FALSE

In the space provided, write "true" if the sentence is true. Write "false" if the sentence is false.

________ 1. Once genes are transferred during gene splicing, they become part of the receiving organism's genes.

________ 2. Genetic engineering is an old technology.

________ 3. Insulin controls growth.

________ 4. New forms of DNA are made in genetic engineering.

________ 5. Genes are made up of DNA.

________ 6. Interferon controls the level of sugar in the blood.

________ 7. A chain of DNA is opened up during gene splicing.

________ 8. Some children do not produce enough human growth hormone.

________ 9. Closing a chain of DNA is the first step of gene splicing.

________ 10. Bacteria are used in genetic engineering.

OTHER GENETIC METHODS

Scientists have other ways to change the genes of organisms besides genetic engineering. Have you ever eaten a seedless orange? Seedless oranges are produced by **cloning.** Cloning is the production of organisms with identical genes. Clones are produced by asexual reproduction.

The first seedless orange tree was the result of a mutation [myoo-TAY-shun]. A mutation is a sudden change in genes. A mutation is an accident. It can cause new inherited traits.

Most mutations occur in nature.

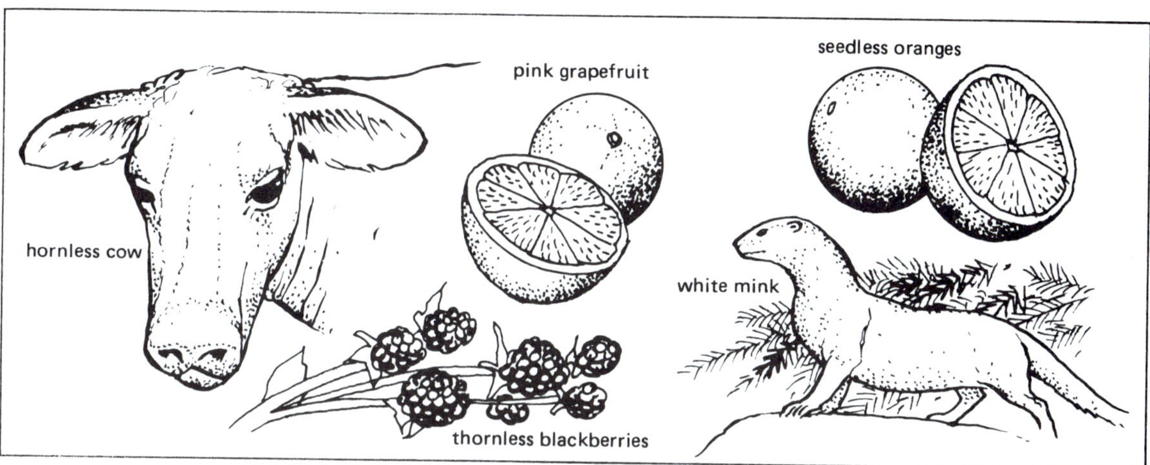

Figure E *Some familiar mutations.*

Figure F *The Mediterraneanean fruit fly damages fruit.*

Scientists can also cause mutations in the laboratory with radiation.

Some male insect pests, like the Mediterranean fruit fly, are given radiation. The radiation causes many changes in the genes. The genes become damaged. With damaged genes, the male flies are sterile.

When the flies mate, no offspring are produced. The insect population is reduced. This is a way of reducing insect pests without harmful chemicals.

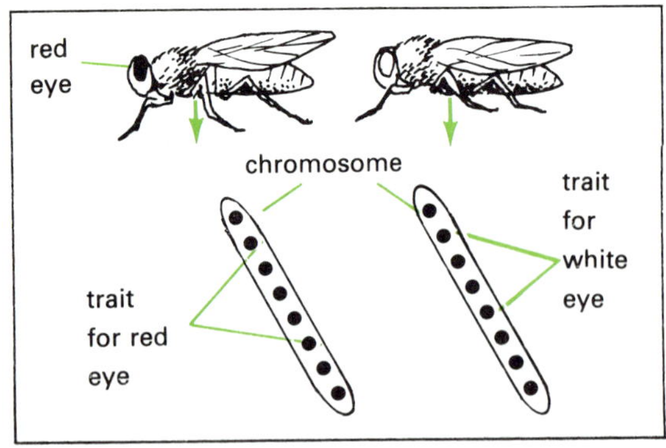

Figure G *White eyes is a mutant trait in fruit flies.*

Mutations also help scientists make a "map" of the chromosomes of the fruit fly.

A chromosome map shows which part of the chromosome controls which trait.

MATCHING

Match each term in Column A with its description in Column B. Write the correct letter in the space provided.

	Column A	Column B
________	**1.** mutation	**a)** production of organisms with identical genes
________	**2.** chromosome map	**b)** can damage genes
________	**3.** radiation	**c)** result of mutation
________	**4.** cloning	**d)** shows which part of the chromosome controls a trait
________	**5.** seedless orange	**e)** sudden change in genes

REACHING OUT

Pieces of DNA that contain DNA from a different organism are called recombinant DNA. Why do you think this a good name?

____

____

____

What is natural selection?

10

evolution [ev-uh-LOO-shun]: process by which organisms change over time
extinct: organism that no longer exists on earth
fossils: remains of organisms that lived in the past
natural selection: survival of organisms with favorable traits

LESSON 10 What is natural selection?

Have you ever visited a natural history museum? If you have, you probably saw some **fossils**. Fossils are the remains of organisms that lived in the past.

Until the 19th century, most scientists believed that organisms lived as they had first appeared on the earth. However, by the late 1700s, scientists had found and studied many fossils. Fossils show interesting things about living things.

Fossils show that organisms have changed. They show that the earliest living things on the earth were simple organisms. In the billions of years that passed, living things became more complex.

Fossils show that many species, or kinds of organisms, died out. These organisms are **extinct.**

Most scientists believe that new species develop from old species as a result of gradual change, or **evolution** [ev-uh-LOO-shun]. Evolution is the process by which organisms change over time.

How and why have living things changed? Different theories of evolution have been given over the years. However, over 100 years ago, an English biologist named Charles Darwin suggested a theory of evolution. Darwin's theory is accepted by most scientists today.

DARWIN'S THEORY OF EVOLUTION

According to Darwin's theory:

1. **OVERPRODUCTION** Organisms produce more offspring than the environment can support. There is not enough food or living space for all of the offspring.

Figure A

2. **COMPETITION** Overproduction leads to a struggle. All the organisms compete for food, water, and the other necessities of life. Only those organisms that are well suited to their surroundings survive and reproduce. The rest die.

Figure B

3. **VARIATIONS** Organisms of the same species are very similar. But they do have individual differences among traits, or variations. These differences are important in the "struggle for survival." For example, extra speed can mean the difference between life and death. A fast gnu may escape an attacking panther. A slower neighbor may become the panther's next meal.

Figure C

4. **SURVIVAL OF THE FIT** Organisms with traits that make them well adapted, or suited to the environment survive and reproduce. Darwin used the term **natural selection** to describe the survival of organisms with favorable traits. They, in turn, pass their favorable traits to their offspring. The offspring are then more likely to survive. As the process of natural selection goes on over many generations, species change. These changes can result in the appearance of a new species. Evolution by natural selection occurs.

Figure D

UNDERSTANDING THE THEORY OF NATURAL SELECTION

Study the diagrams. Then, answer the questions.

1. According to Darwin, did all ancient giraffes have long necks.

   ____

Figure E

2. ________________ -necked giraffes
   (Long, Short)

   were better able to reach food far off the ground.

3. ________________ -necked giraffes were better suited to the environment.

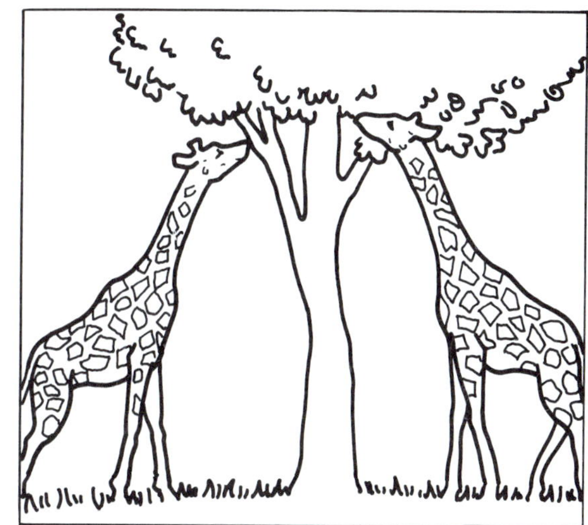

Figure F

4. The ________________ -necked
   (long, short)

   giraffes died out.

5. Which giraffes survived and reproduced?

   The ________________ -necked
   (long, short)

   giraffes.

6. What important adaptation did the surviving giraffes pass on to their offspring.

   ____

7. Describe the necks of all giraffes living today (HINT: One word will do)

   ____

Figure G

FILL IN THE BLANK

Complete each statement using a term or terms from the list below. Write your answers in the spaces provided.

changing	favorable	organisms
Charles Darwin	adapted	competition
variations	different	limited number
extinct	reproduce	

1. An organism that is suited to its environment is said to be ________________ to its surroundings.
2. Earth is always ________________ .
3. As the earth changes, the ________________ that live on it also change.
4. A species that does not change as its environment changes may become ________________ .
5. The scientist who developed an important theory of evolution was ________________ .

ACCORDING TO DARWIN:

6. A favorable environment can support only a ________________ of organisms.
7. Overproduction leads to ________________ .
8. Organisms belonging to the same species can have ________________ traits.
9. Differences among traits are called ________________ .
10. Organisms that are adapted to their environment ________________ and pass their ________________ traits on to their offspring.

What evidence supports evolution?

11

anatomy [uh-NAT-uh-mee]: study of the parts, or structures, of living things
vestigial [ves-TIJ-ee-uhl] **structures:** body parts that are reduced in size and that serve no function

LESSON 11 | What evidence supports evolution?

Imagine that you were a "spy" looking for clues to support evolution. Where would you look? There is evidence for evolution from the following different areas:

FOSSIL EVIDENCE A fossil is the remains, or traces, of organisms that lived long ago. The fossil record shows that organisms have changed over time. It shows that the earliest organisms were simple living things. They lived in water. Fossils show that these organisms evolved into more complex organisms over millions of years.

ANATOMY The study of the parts, or structures, of living things is called **anatomy** [uh-NAT-uh-mee]. By studing the parts of living things, we can find out how closely related they are. For example, the bones of a bat's wing and a human hand are similar. This suggests the animals are related.

Can you wiggle your ears? It's always good for a laugh, but nothing else, at least for modern humans. Ear movements are controlled by muscles. Human ear muscles are considered **vestigial** [ves-TIJ-ee-uhl] **structures**. Vestigial structures are "left overs." They are usually reduced in size and serve no function. Scientists think vestigial structures had a function in the ancestors of animals that now have them. Almost all animals have vestigial structures. Humans have more than 100. The appendix is another human vestigial structure.

EMBRYOLOGY An embryo is an organism in its very early stages of development, <u>before</u> it is born. Embryology is the study of embryos <u>as</u> they develop. Scientists compare the embryos of different living things to see if they are alike. Organisms with similar embryos probably evolved from a common ancestor.

BIOCHEMISTRY All living things are made up of chemicals called proteins. There are many kinds of proteins. Each has its own chemical "print" or structures. Scientists can identify the chemical make-up of proteins. They have discovered that the blood of certain animals have particular kinds of proteins. They compare the blood proteins of different animals. In this way, they can tell how closely the organisms are related.

MORE ABOUT FOSSIL EVIDENCE

- Most fossils are found in layered rocks.
- Lower layers were layed down first. They are older than the layers above them.
- Fossils found in the lower layers are older than fossils found in the upper layers.

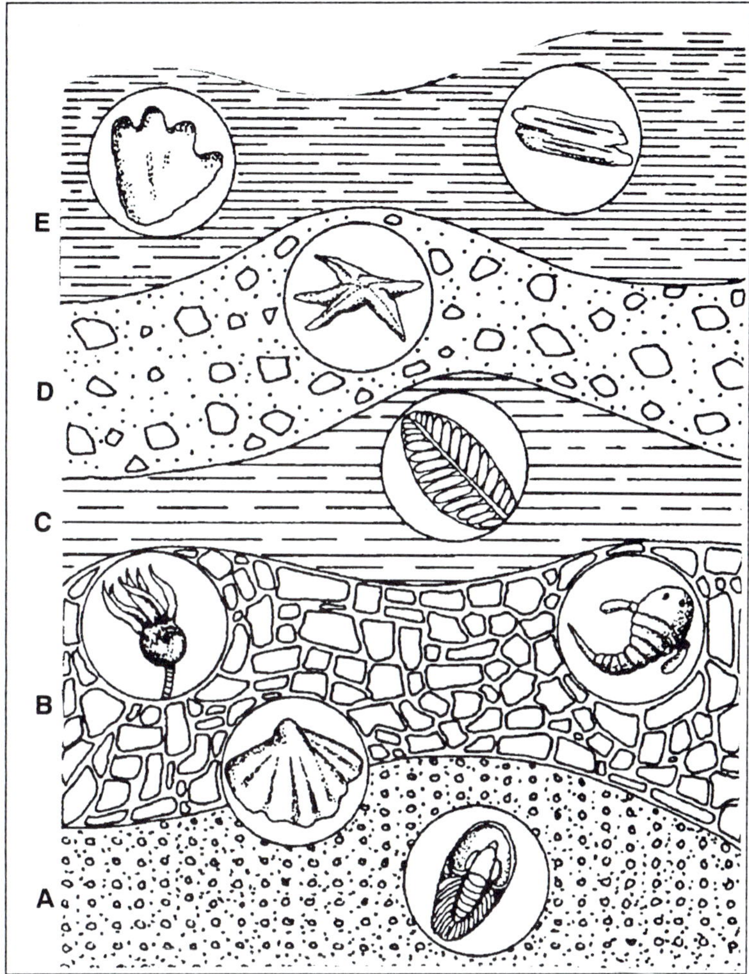

Figure A

Figure A shows five rock layers. Each contains fossils.

Study the layers and then answer the questions.

1. Which rock layer is the oldest? ________________

2. Which rock layer is the youngest? ________________

3. Which layer has the oldest fossils? ________________

4. Which layer has the youngest fossils? ________________

5. a) Fossils found in layer C are ________________ than fossils found in layers D and E.
   older, younger

   b) Fossils found in layer C are ________________ than fossils found in A and B.
   older, younger

EVOLUTION OF THE HORSE

The first horse appeared about 60 million years ago. Since that time, it has been changing. Study Figure B. What changes do you see? Fill in the correct answers.

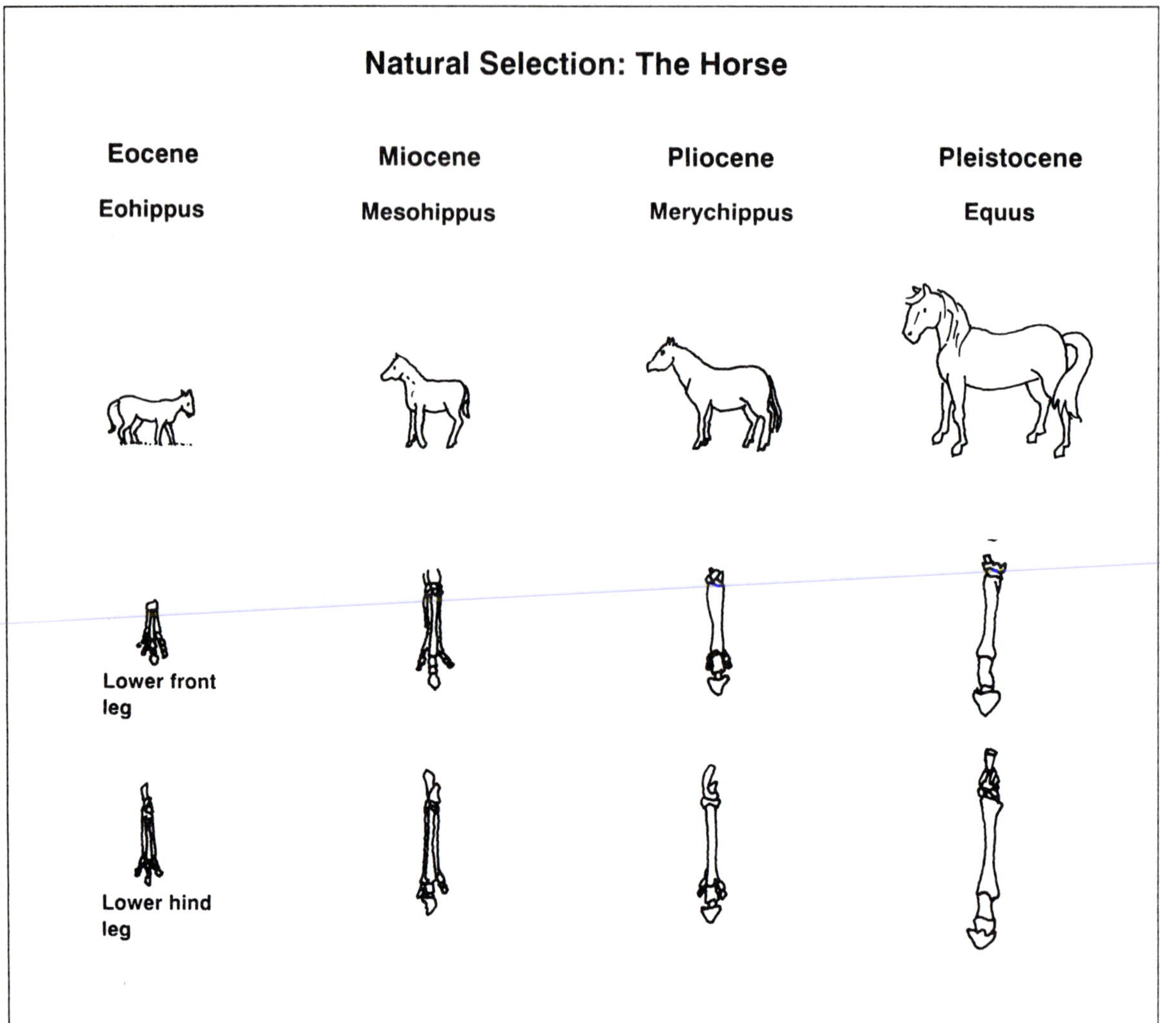

Figure B

1. What happened to the size of the horse? ________________________

2. The earliest horse had ________________ toes.
   one, many

3. How many toes does a modern horse have? ________________ What is it called? (Use your own experience.) ________________

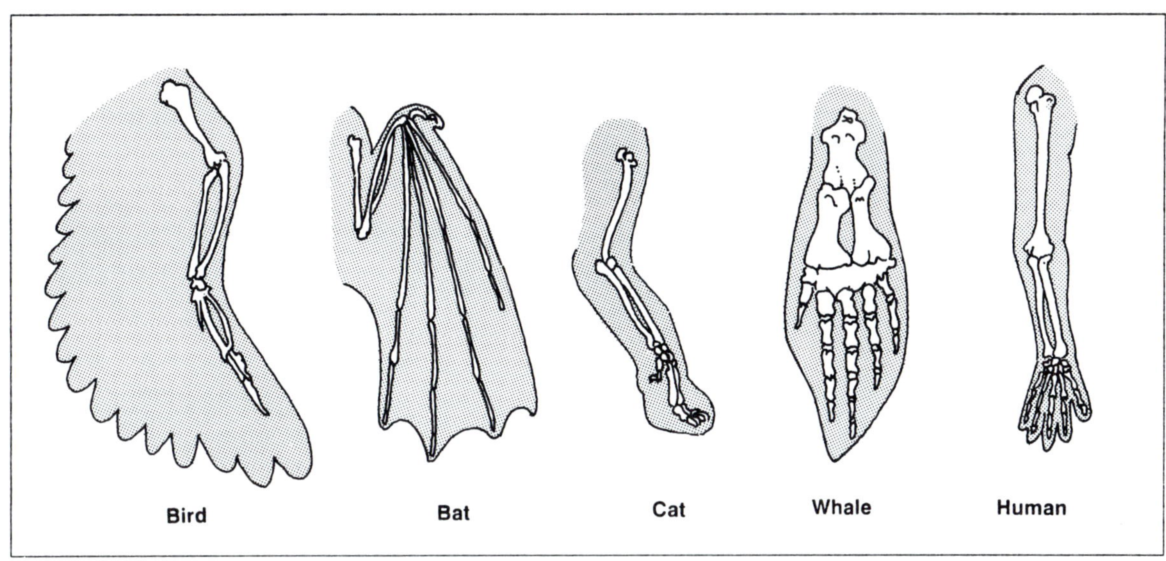

Figure C

Figure C shows the wing of a bird, the wing of a bat, the foreleg of a cat, the flipper of a whale, and the hand and arm of a human. On the outside, they look very different. However, inside the bones are very similar. The bones are arranged in similar ways. They develop in much the same way.

1. Anatomy shows that these animals ________________ (do, do not) have a close ancestor.

Figure D

The wings of a bee and the wings of a bird have the same function. Both are used for flying. However, their anatomy shows that their wings are very different. They develop in totally different ways.

2. Anatomy shows that birds and bees are ________________ (distant, close) relatives.

3. Birds and bees ________________ (did, did not) develop along the same evolutionary "branch."

EMBRYOLOGY

The similarity of some organisms shows that they probably evolved from a common ancestor.

Figure E shows the development of a **fish**, a **turtle**, a **chicken**, a **pig**, and a **human**. Study the pictures and then answer the questions.

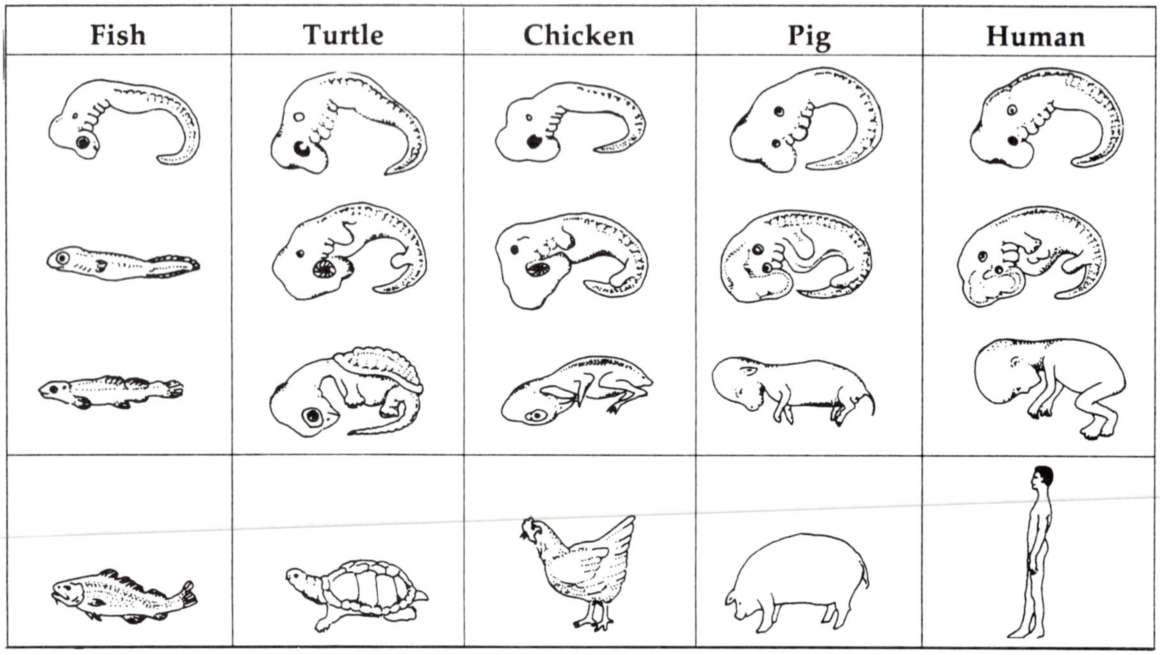

Fish	Turtle	Chicken	Pig	Human

Figure E

1. The adults look very ________________ .
   similar, different

2. The earliest embryos look very ________________ .
   similar, different

________ 3. Which organisms are the <u>most</u> closely related?

a) chickens and humans   b) fish and pigs

c) pigs and humans   d) turtles and pigs

________ 4. Which organisms are the <u>least</u> closely related?

a) fish and turtles   b) pigs and chickens

c) fish and humans   d) pigs and humans

5. Embryos that are <u>most</u> alike are those that are the ________________ closely related.
   most, least

6. Embryos that are <u>least</u> alike are those that are the ________________ closely related.
   most, least

TRUE OR FALSE

In the space provided, write "true" if the sentence is true. Write "false" if the sentence is false.

_________ 1. Fossils found in upper rock layers are older than fossils found in lower layers.

_________ 2. Structure means how something is used.

_________ 3. Function means how something is used.

_________ 4. Different animals with parts that have similar structure and function are probably distant relatives.

_________ 5. Embryology is the study of adult organisms.

_________ 6. Closely related embryos look more alike - and for a longer time, than embryos of distant relatives.

_________ 7. The most complete fossil record is of the horse.

_________ 8. The wings of bees and birds are very similar.

_________ 9. Vestigial organs have no functions.

_________ 10. Blood proteins can show evolutionary relationships.

NOW TRY THIS

Read each statement. Indicate whether each statement uses anatomy (A), biochemistry (B), or embryology (E) as evidence of evolutionary relationships among organisms. Write the correct letter in the space provided.

_________ 1. The forelimbs of a penguin and alligator have similar bone structures.

_________ 2. The early stages of development in a fish, a rabbit, and a gorilla look alike.

_________ 3. In the wing of a bat and the arm of a human, you find bones calld the radius, humerus, and ulna.

_________ 4. Some blood proteins are found in almost all organisms.

_________ 5. The finger bones in mammals have the same structure.

FILL IN THE BLANK

Complete each statement using a term or terms from the list below. Write your answers in the spaces provided. Some words may be used more than once.

fossil	layered	function
blood	vestigial	development
four	proteins	ancestor

1. In humans, the tailbone is a ________________ structure.
2. An embryo is an organism in its early stages of ________________.
3. All living things have chemicals called ________________ .
4. The wings of birds and bats show that these organisms probably have a common ________________.
5. The most complete ________________ record is of the horse.
6. Most fossils are found in ________________ rocks.
7. Organisms with similar embryos probably evolved from a common ________________ .
8. The ________________ of certain animals has particular kinds of proteins.
9. Vestigial structures have no ________________ .
10. The earliest horse had ________________ toes.

REACHING OUT

The appendix is a small outgrowth at the lower part of the large intestine. In some plant eating animals, it is much larger — and is important in digestion.

Sometimes, a person's appendix becomes infected and is removed. Surgeons have removed millions of appendixes. No bad side-effects have been noted after its removal.

What does this prove? ____

____

____

EVOLUTION

How does adaptation help species survive?

12

adaptation [ad-up-TAY-shun]: trait of an organism that helps it live in its environment
camouflage [KAM-uh-flahj]: ability of an organism to blend in with its surroundings
mimicry [MIM-ik-ree]: adaptation of an organism that protects the organism because its appearance is similar to another organism

LESSON 12 | How does adaptation help a species survive?

An organism must be well suited to its environment in order to survive. It must be able to tolerate the climate. It must also be able to get food, protect itself from enemies, and reproduce. An organism that is well suited to its environment is said to be adapted to its environment. In Lessons 10 and 11, you learned that organisms that are adapted to their environment have a better chance of surviving and reproducing.

Any trait of an organism that helps it live in its environment is called an **adaptation** [ad-up-TAY-shun]. Adaptations make each kind of living thing able to live in its environment. They allow one kind of organism to live where others cannot.

For example, polar bears live unprotected in sub-zero weather. You cannot. Neither can most organisms. Polar bears are "built" for the bitter cold. They have a thick layer of fat and dense fur to keep them warm.

Some animals live comfortably in other climates. The camel, for example, is suited to live in the hot, dry desert. Alligators are suited to live in hot, humid marshes.

Adaptation applies not only to animals. It applies to plants and other groups of living things as well. For example, a cactus can grow in the hot, dry desert. An oak tree, on the other hand, grows well in a cooler, moister environment.

Earth is about 4 1/2 billion years old. Life has existed here for more than one billion years. Fossil records tell us that Earth has been constantly changing. So have its life forms.

Many species that lived in the past have died out. They are extinct. These organisms could not adapt to their changing environments.

MORE ABOUT ADAPTATION

Adaptation may take many forms. Here are a few examples.

The woodpecker is well adapted to dig insects out of trees.

Figure A

Birds have feathers and lightweight bones. They are well adapted for flight.

Can you think of a better way to escape an attacker? Fly away and live to fly another day.

Figure B

The streamline shape of fish allow them to move quickly through the water.

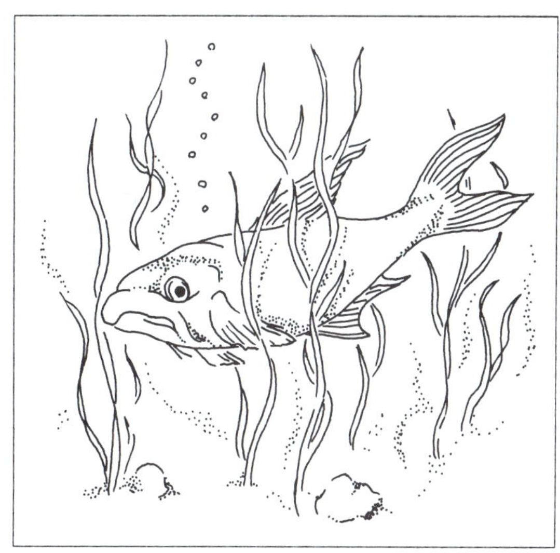

Figure C

Some organisms adapt by looking like other organisms. For example, the monarch butterfly (top) is "bad tasting."

The viceroy butterfly (bottom) is not bad tasting. Hunting birds do not know this. They are fooled by the look-alike butterfly. So they stay away from both species.

This adaptation is called **mimicry** [MIM-ik-ree].

Figure D

Some organisms blend in with their surroundings. This makes it difficult for other organisms to see them . . .

See how this toad blends in with its surroundings. It is almost invisible.

Figure E

The polar bear and the snowy owl blend in with the white arctic snow.

This adaptation is called **camouflage** [KAM-uh-flahj].

Figure F

BIRD ADAPTATIONS

The beaks and feet of birds are examples of adaptation.

Look at the diagrams of the feet and beaks of different kinds of birds. Then see if you can match the diagrams with the descriptions that follow. Place the correct letter on the lines provided.

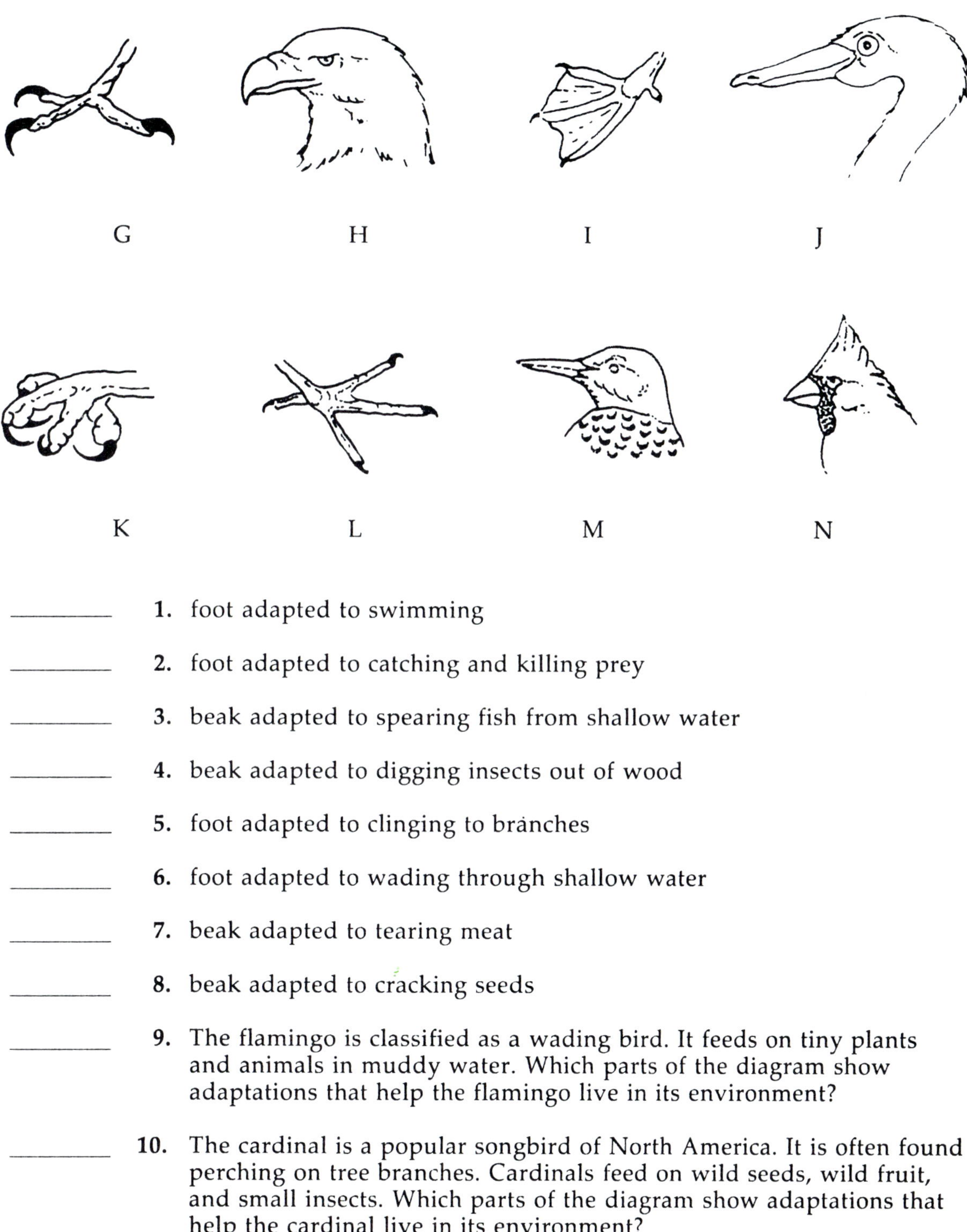

_________ **1.** foot adapted to swimming

_________ **2.** foot adapted to catching and killing prey

_________ **3.** beak adapted to spearing fish from shallow water

_________ **4.** beak adapted to digging insects out of wood

_________ **5.** foot adapted to clinging to branches

_________ **6.** foot adapted to wading through shallow water

_________ **7.** beak adapted to tearing meat

_________ **8.** beak adapted to cracking seeds

_________ **9.** The flamingo is classified as a wading bird. It feeds on tiny plants and animals in muddy water. Which parts of the diagram show adaptations that help the flamingo live in its environment?

_________ **10.** The cardinal is a popular songbird of North America. It is often found perching on tree branches. Cardinals feed on wild seeds, wild fruit, and small insects. Which parts of the diagram show adaptations that help the cardinal live in its environment?

WORD SEARCH

The list on the left contains words that you have used in this Lesson. Find and circle each word where it appears in the box. The spellings may go in any direction: up, down, left, right, or diagonally.

adapt
blend
cactus
camouflage
extinct
mimicry
species
suited
survive
viceroy

S	A	T	E	V	M	V	O	A	E
P	U	B	H	V	C	G	W	G	N
E	X	T	I	N	C	T	A	S	S
C	D	T	S	N	A	L	X	U	U
I	X	R	F	Z	F	Y	T	I	R
E	T	L	B	U	D	C	K	T	V
S	D	Q	O	L	A	N	P	E	I
M	I	M	I	C	R	Y	E	D	V
T	A	D	A	P	T	I	J	L	E
C	G	V	I	C	E	R	0	Y	B

What are the characteristics of primates?

13

bipedal [by-PEED-uhl]: upright; walk on two legs instead of four
opposable thumb: a thumb that can touch all of the other fingers
primates: order of mammals

LESSON 13 What are the characteristics of primates?

What do tree shrews, lemurs, monkeys, apes, and humans have in common? They are all **primates**. Primates make up an order of mammals.

Early primates lived in trees. Most modern primates also live in trees. So, does it surprise you that primates have many characteristics that help them live in trees? It should not. These characteristics are adaptations to life in the trees.

All primates have flexible fingers and toes. Their fingers and toes have nails instead of claws. Some primates use their movable fingers and toes to grasp branches.

Most primates also have an **opposable thumb.** An opposable thumb can touch all of the other fingers. Touch all your other fingers with your thumb. You can see that humans have opposable thumbs too.

All primates have eyes in the front of their head. This lets them look at an object with both eyes at the same time.

Primates also have large brains compared to their body size. A large brain does not always mean greater intelligence. But, a large brain may have helped early primates adapt and survive.

HUMAN CHARACTERISTICS

Humans have all of the characteristics of other primates. They also have some characteristics that set them apart.

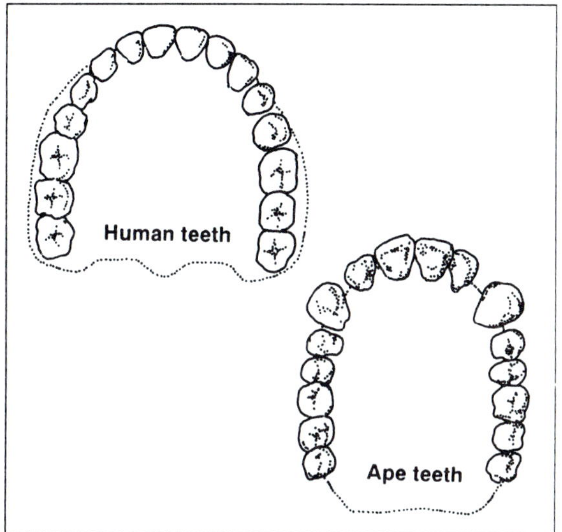

Figure A

The jaws and teeth of humans are different from other primates. The human jaw is more rounded in shape. The rows of teeth in an ape's jaw form a "U". That is why an ape's jaw sticks out from its face. A human jaw does not.

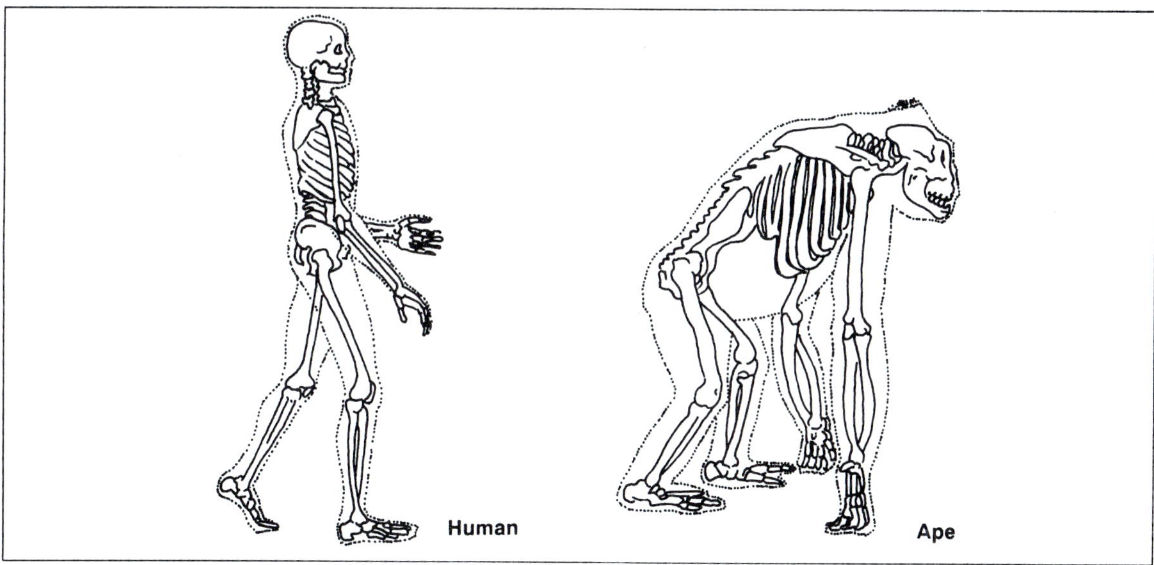

Figure B

Humans are **bipedal** [by-PEED-uhl]. Being bipedal means that humans stand upright. They walk on two legs instead of four.

Look at Figure B. You can see that an ape's pelvic bones are adapted for walking on all fours. The human pelvis allows humans to walk on two legs.

Figure C

Humans have large brains. The human brain is more highly developed than the brains of other primates.

The large front part of the brain is responsible for spoken language. Humans are the only animals that use spoken language to communicate with one another.

NOW TRY THIS

*Write **H** if the characteristic refers only to humans. Write **P** of the characteristic refers to humans and most other primates.*

_______ **1.** Opposite thumb

_______ **2.** Frontal vision

_______ **3.** Bipedal

_______ **4.** Flexible fingers

_______ **5.** Toes with nails instead of claws

_______ **6.** Walking upright on two legs

_______ **7.** Curved jaw that does not stick out from the face

_______ **8.** Spoken language

PRIMATE OR HUMAN?

*Compare the skulls in Figures D and E and the jaws in Figures F and G. Decide which is a human skull and jaw and which is an ape skull and jaw. Write either **primate** or **human** on the lines provided. Then give reasons for your answers.*

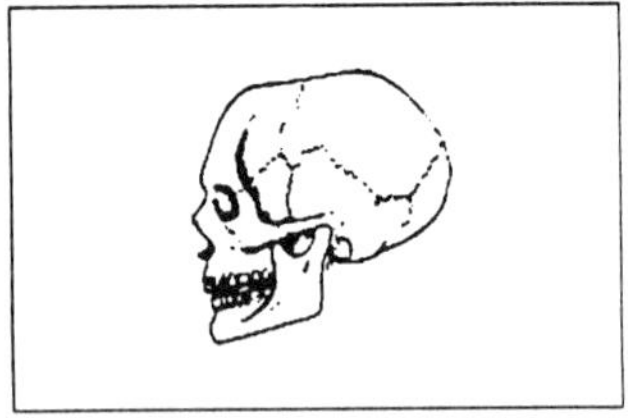

Figure D

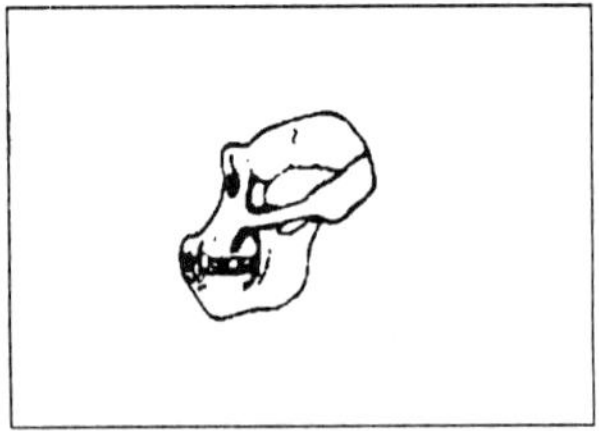

Figure E

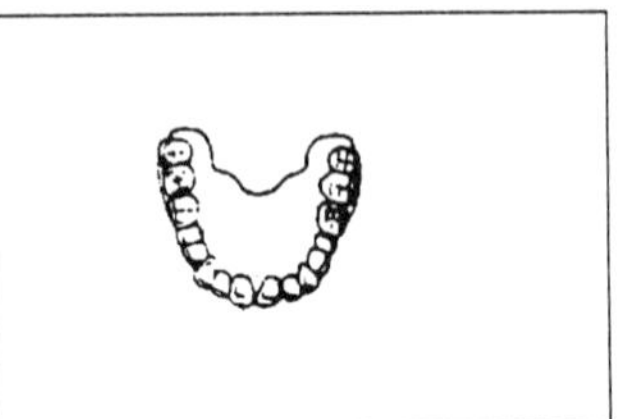

Figure F

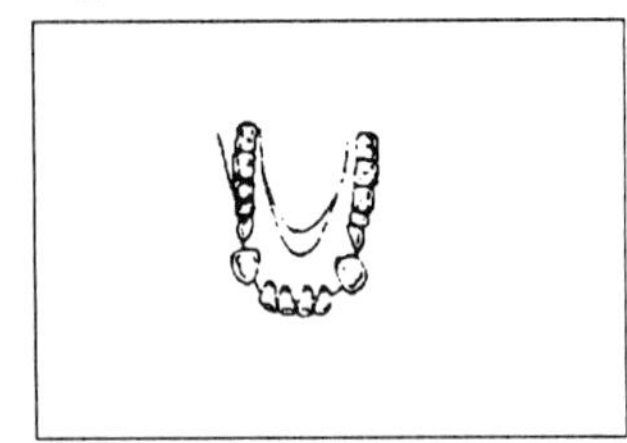

Figure G

D. _______________

E. _______________

F. _______________

G. _______________

Reasons: ____

____

IMPORTANCE OF AN OPPOSABLE THUMB

How important is your thumb? More important than you may realize...

Figure H

TRY THIS:

Tape your right thumb (if you are right-handed) to your next finger. Then try to do these tasks....

1. Fasten (or unfasten) a button.
2. Pick up a book.
3. Turn a doorknob.
4. Hold an object as you would a hammer.
5. Turn a screwdriver.

How important is the thumb? You answer the question!

Do you think civilization would be as advanced if people did not have thumbs?

____

Explain your answer. ____

____

TRUE OR FALSE

In the space provided, write "true" if the sentence is true. Write "false" if the sentence is false.

________ **1.** Most modern primates live in trees.

________ **2.** Primates have claws instead of nails.

________ **3.** A large brain always means greater intelligence.

________ **4.** All primates have flexible fingers and toes.

________ **5.** All primates are bipedal.

________ **6.** Only humans have frontal vision.

________ **7.** Early primates lived in trees.

________ **8.** Most primates have an opposable thumb.

________ **9.** Apes and humans are the only animals that use spoken language to communicate.

________ **10.** Tree shrews and lemurs are primates.

WORD SCRAMBLE

Below are several scrambled words you have used in this Lesson. Unscramble the words and write your answers in the spaces provided.

1. BINRA ________________

2. ERTSE ________________

3. PESA ________________

4. MHTBU ________________

5. SPERTIMA ________________

How did humans evolve?

14

anthropologists [an-thruh-PAHL-uh-jists]: scientists who study human beings and trace their evolution

hominids [HOM-uh-nids]: group of primates in which modern humans and their ancestors are classified

LESSON 14 How did humans evolve?

Apes, chimpanzees, monkeys, tree shrews—in Lesson 13 you learned that all of these animals are primates. Humans are primates too. Modern humans and their ancestors are classified in a group of primates called **hominids** [HOM-uh-nids].

The fossil record of human evolution is not complete. **Anthropologists** [an-thruh-PAHL-uh-jists] are still looking for clues to human evolution. Anthropologists are scientists who study human beings and trace their evolution.

The oldest fossils of hominids have been found in Africa. These fossils show that the earliest hominids walked upright and were about 1 meter tall. The fossils range from about 2 1/2 to 3 1/2 million years old.

Later humanlike fossils also have been found. Fossils of each species show more humanlike traits and behaviors than the species that lived before them. For example, they show an increase in body size. They have larger skulls too. Some of the later species used tools. Others lived in caves, used fire, and hunted for food.

Modern humans belong to the species *Homo sapiens* [SAY-pee-uhns]. this means "wise human". Fossils of two earlier types of modern humans have been found. They are called Neanderthals [nee-AN-dur-thals] and Cro-Magnons [kroh-MAG-nunz]. You will learn more about these two types of *Homo sapiens* on the following pages.

NEANDERTHALS

The first fossils of *Homo sapiens* were found in the Neander Valley of Germany. These were called Neanderthals [nee-AN-dur-thawls]. The Neanderthals lived from 130,000 to 35,000 years ago. They lived during the Ice Age in Europe.

Figure A

Neanderthals were somewhat shorter than modern humans. They walked upright. They had large skulls with sloping foreheads and heavy brow bones. They had large brains.

Their large brains help Neanderthals adapt to the cold Ice Age. They lived in caves and used fire to keep warm. The Neanderthals also were the first people known to bury their dead.

CRO-MAGNONS

The fossils of Cro-Magnons [kroh-MAG-nuhnz] were found in a cave in France. These fossils were about 35,000 years old.

Cro-Magnons had high foreheads and no brow ridges. They looked like modern humans.

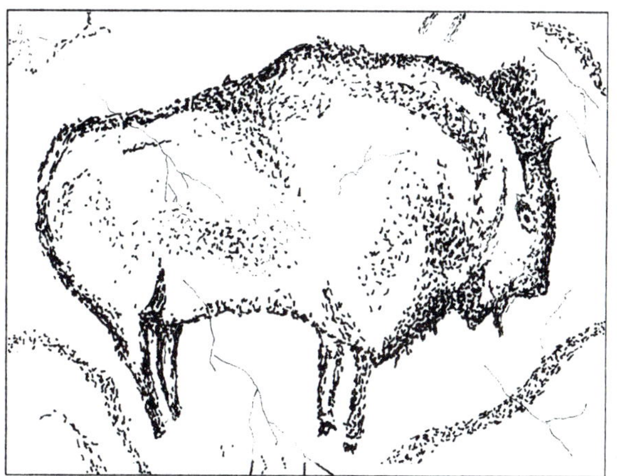

Figure B

Scientists have found evidence that Cro-Magnons were skilled hunters and tool makers. They also made sculptures and paintings on the walls of their caves.

NEANDERTHAL OR CRO-MAGNON

*Decide whether the statements below refer to a Cro-Magnon or a Neanderthal. In the spaces provided, write **C** if the statement refers to a Cro-Magnon or **N** of it refers to a Neanderthal.*

_________ **1.** sloping foreheads and heavy brow bones

_________ **2.** looked like modern humans

_________ **3.** first *Homo sapiens* known to bury their dead

_________ **4.** shorter than modern humans

_________ **5.** made paintings on cave walls

Answer the following.

1. What does "*Homo sapiens*" Mean? _________________________

2. What is anthropology? _________________________

3. How do you think scientists discovered that Cro-Magnons were skilled hunters and toolmakers? _________________________

____

4. Name two types of early humans. _________________________

____

EVOLUTIONARY CHANGES IN HUMANS

We know about human development from studying fossil bones.

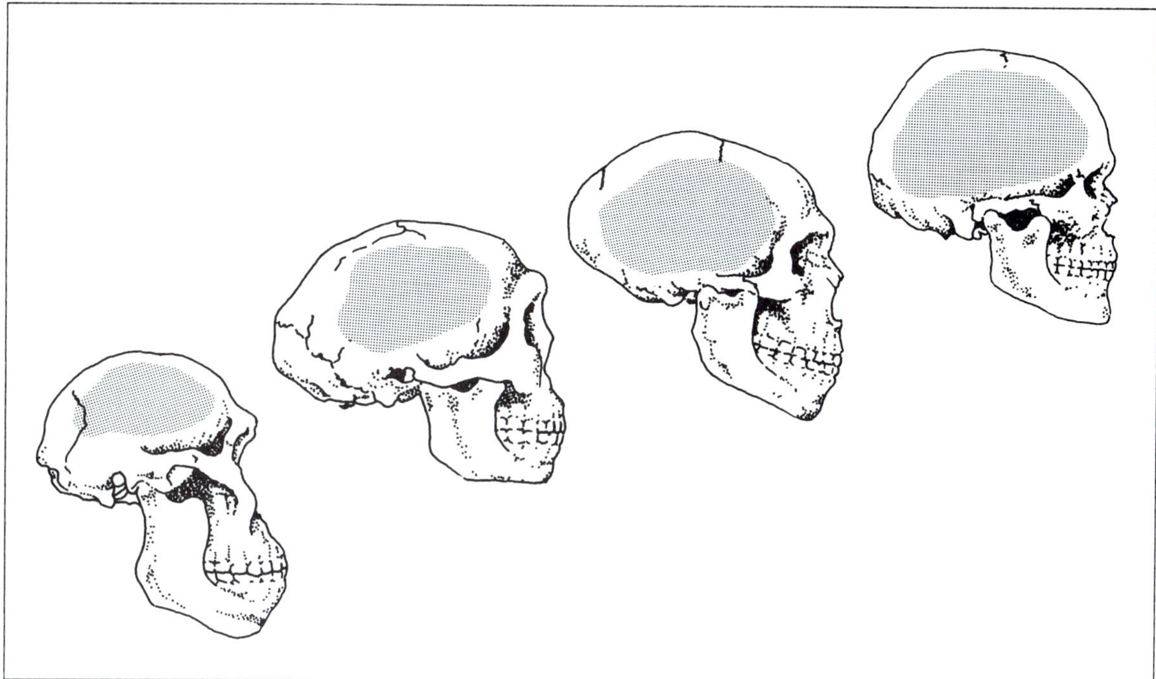

Figure C

Figure C shows four stages of human skull development—from the first man-ape to modern human.

Imagine you are an anthropologist. Compare skulls carefully. Then answers the questions below.

As humans developed:

1. Their brain size ______________________________ .
increased, decreased

2. The skull became ______________________________ .
larger, smaller

3. The skull also became ______________________________ .
less rounded, more rounded

4. The jaw moved ______________________________ .
forward, back

5. The bony brow ridge ______________________________ .
extended even more, became smaller

OTHER EVOLUTIONARY CHANGES

Study the diagrams below and then answer the questions.

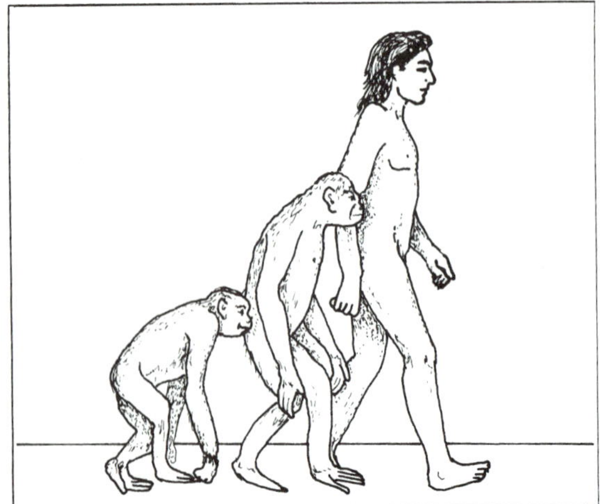

Figure D

Modern human | Middle hominid | Early hominid

Figure E

1. As humans developed,

   a) <u>posture</u> became ______________ erect.
   (more, less)

   b) the <u>head</u> dropped ______________ .
   (more, less)

2. The <u>body</u> had ______________ hair.
   (more, less)

3. The <u>"eye" teeth</u> (canines) became ______________ .
   (smaller, larger)

4. The <u>mouth</u> (not lips) became more ______________ .
   ("u" shaped, rounded)

NOW TRY AND ANSWER THESE

5. <u>Reasoning power</u> ______________________________ .
   (improved, remained the same, became worse)

6. <u>Ability to communicate</u> ______________________________ .
   (improved, remained the same, became worse)

7. <u>Coordination</u> ______________________________ .
   (improved, remained the same, became worse)

8. There is <u>one</u> main reason for your answers to questions 5, 6, and 7.

   What is that reason? ____

MATCHING SKULLS WITH HEADS

Four skulls and four heads are shown below. They are not matched. Match each skull to its correct head. Write your answers in the chart below.

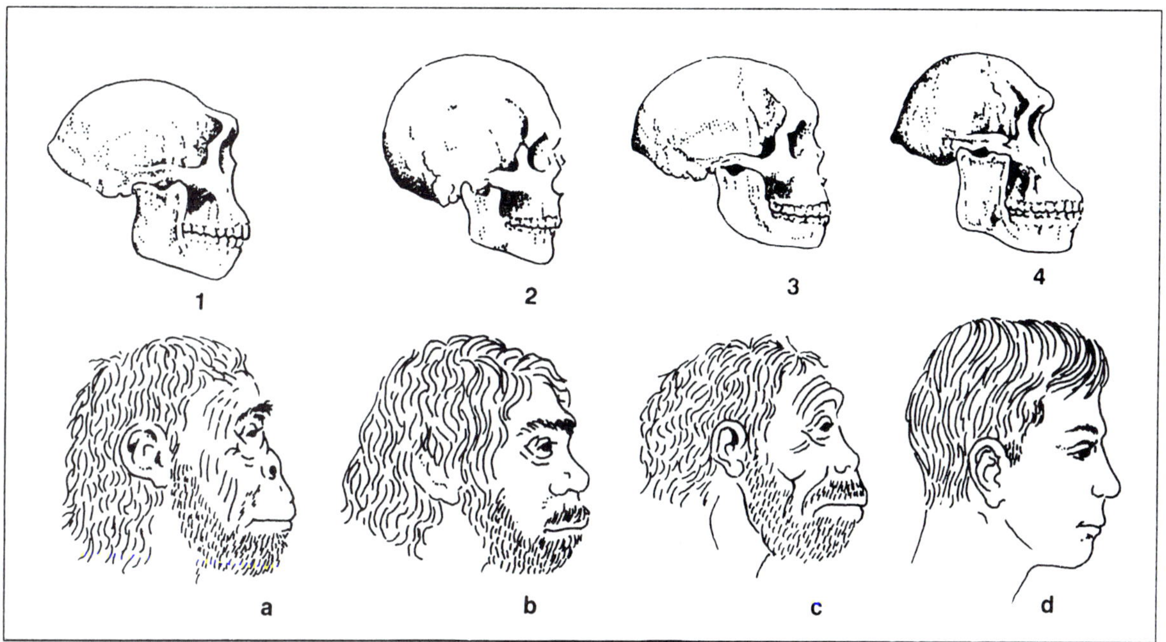

Figure F

SKULL	MATCHING HEAD
1	
2	
3	
4	

1. Now arrange the pairs according to <u>advancing</u> evolution.

   (Earliest pair first) ______________________________

2. Which was the least developed skull? ______________________________
3. How do you know? ______________________________
4. Which was the most developed skull? ______________________________
5. How do you know? ______________________________

FILL IN THE BLANK

Complete each statement using a term or terms from the list below. Write your answers in the spaces provided. Some words may be used more than once.

most advanced	primates	Germany
largest	complete	hominids
fossil bones	anthropologists	humans

1. Apes, chimps, monkeys, and humans are classified as ______________ .
2. Primates are the ______________ of all animals.
3. The most intelligent primates are ______________ .
4. Relative to their size, humans have the ______________ brain.
5. Scientists who study human development are called ____________________ .
6. Modern humans and their ancestors are classified as ______________ .
7. The only surviving hominids are ______________ .
8. The fossil record of human evolution is not ______________ .
9. Most of what we know about human evolution has come from studying

 ______________ .
10. The first fossils of modern humans were found in ______________ .

WORD SCRAMBLE

Below are several scrambled words you have used in this Lesson. Unscramble the words and write your answers in the spaces provided.

1. SNAHUM ____________________
2. CEVAS ____________________
3. PSIMRTAE ____________________
4. SHOINIMD ____________________
5. LKUSL ____________________

TRUE OR FALSE

In the space provided, write "true" if the sentence is true. Write "false" if the sentence is false.

_________ **1.** The oldest fossils of hominids have been found in Africa

_________ **2.** Hominids include apes, monkeys, and humans.

_________ **3.** The earliest hominids were as tall as modern humans.

_________ **4.** *Homo sapiens* means "wise human."

_________ **5.** All modern humans belong to the species *Homo sapiens.*

_________ **6.** Neanderthal fossils were first found in a cave in France

_________ **7.** Cro-Magnons were skilled hunters and tool makers.

_________ **8.** Neanderthals lived during the Ice Age.

_________ **9.** Cro-Magnons were the first people known to bury their dead.

_________ **10.** Fossils of each hominid species show more humanlike traits than the species that lived before them.

REACHING OUT

The words *Homo sapien* mean "wise human." Why do you think scientists gave this name to this group of hominids? ____________________

____

____

____

SCIENCE *EXTRA*

The Chimpanzee—Human Link

Is the chimpanzee the closest living relative of humans? Some scientists who study DNA say that the chimpanzee and humans are each other's closest relative. Other scientists who study the bone anatomy of apes and humans say the gorilla and the chimpanzee are each other's closest relative. Who is right?

Scientists who study DNA have found laboratory methods for comparing the DNA from different species. In one method, scientists figure out the sequence of building blocks that make up DNA in two species. They then compare these sequences to each other.

In another method, scientists mix short strands of DNA from two species together. Sometimes the DNA building blocks from one species will attach to DNA building blocks from the second species. When this happens, the scientists can measure the strength of this attachment. The stronger the attachment, the more closely related the two species are. These scientists say their results show that DNA from humans and chimps is nearly identical, indicating a very close relationship.

The scientists who study bone size and shape point out many physical similarities between gorillas and chimps that are not present in humans. One of these similarities is knuckle-walking, which means that when the apes walk on all fours, they walk on their knuckles, not their palms. If chimps and humans are each other's closest living relatives, might there be evidence that human ancestors used knuckle-walking too?

Another close similarity between the two great apes is the structure of their teeth. These two pieces of evidence are used to support a closer relationship between gorillas and chimps.

All scientists agree on one important point: chimps, gorillas, and humans share a common ancestor. They disagree, however, on whether modern gorilla's ancestors split from this evolutionary line before the human-chimp ancestor, or whether the human line split off leaving a common ancestor for chimps and gorillas.

Who will win the argument? It is quite possible that research in the next few years will settle this question.

What are viruses?

15

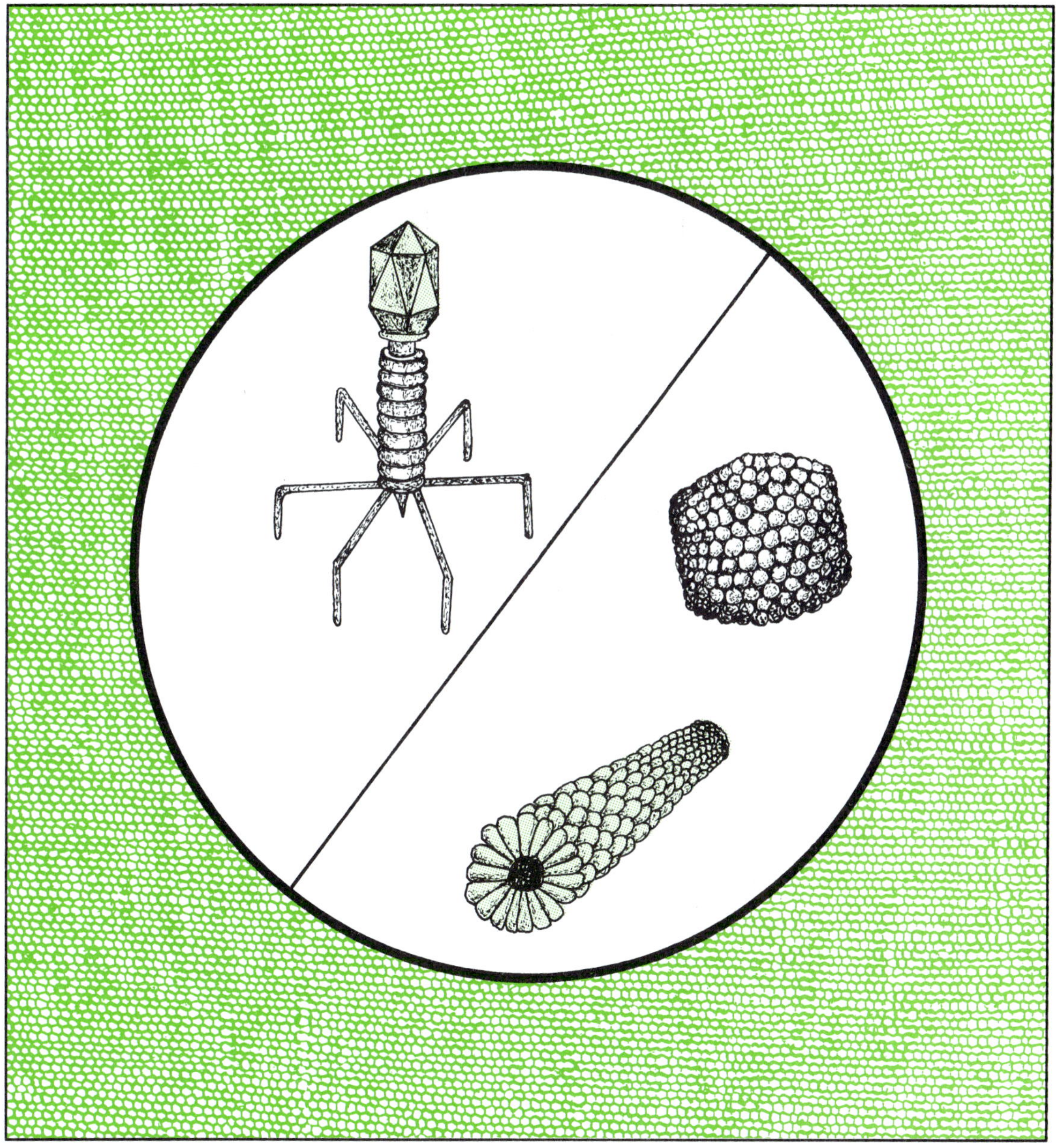

capsid [KAP-sid]: coat of protein that covers a virus
nucleic [new-KLEE-ik] **acids**: organic compounds that make proteins, control the cell, and determine heredity
virus: piece of nucleic acid covered with an outercoat of protein

LESSON 15 | What are viruses?

Alive or not alive? That is the question! Scientists do not agree about whether viruses are actually living things.

Viruses are unusual. A virus has no cell parts. A **virus** is just made up of a substance called **nucleic** [new-KLEE-ik] **acid** covered by an "over-coat" of protein. The outer coat is called a **capsid** [KAP-sid]. The capsid makes up most of the virus.

Capsids gives viruses their shapes. Some viruses are round. Others look like long rods. Some have very unusual shapes. You can see the shapes of some viruses in Figure A on the facing page.

How else does a virus differ from living cells? A virus does not ingest or digest food. It does not carry out respiration. In fact, a virus does not carry out any of the life processes except reproduction—and then, only when it is inside another living cell. When a virus is outside a living cell, it is just a "chemical." What happens when a virus infects a cell? it may cause disease. Viruses cause many diseases in plants and animals. When you have the "flu," you are infected with a virus.

Because viruses do not have all the characteristics of living things, they are not classified in the five kingdoms. Instead, most scientists classify viruses according to the living things they infect. The three main groups are: plant viruses, animal viruses and bacterial viruses.

Viruses are ultra-small. Bacteria are tiny. Yet, compared to viruses, bacteria are giants! Think of this....a single microscopic cell may contain millions of virus particles.

MORE ABOUT VIRUSES

Figure A

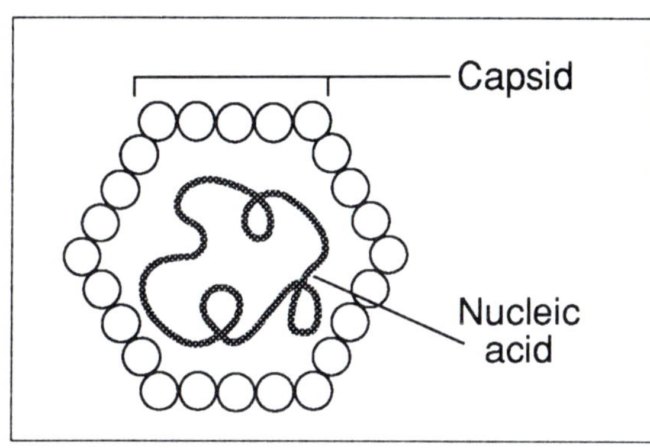

Figure B

1. The two parts of a virus are __________ and a __________ .
2. Which part makes up most of a virus? ____________________
3. Which part gives a virus its shape? ____________________
4. How do viruses differ from living cells? ____
5. What is the only life function that a virus carries out? ____________________
6. When is the only time this life process can take place? ____
7. How do most scientists classify viruses? ____
8. What are the three main groups of viruses? ____

REPRODUCTION IN VIRUSES

When a virus enters a cell, it takes over the cell and causes it to make new viruses. Scientists first learned about how viruses reproduce by studying bacterial viruses.

As you read about how viruses reproduce, look at Figure C.

1. A virus attaches to a cell.
2. The virus sends its nucleic acid into the cell. The capsid stays outside.
3. The virus takes over the cell. It directs the cell to make new viruses.
4. The new viruses burst out of the cell. This kills the cell. The new viruses attack other cells.

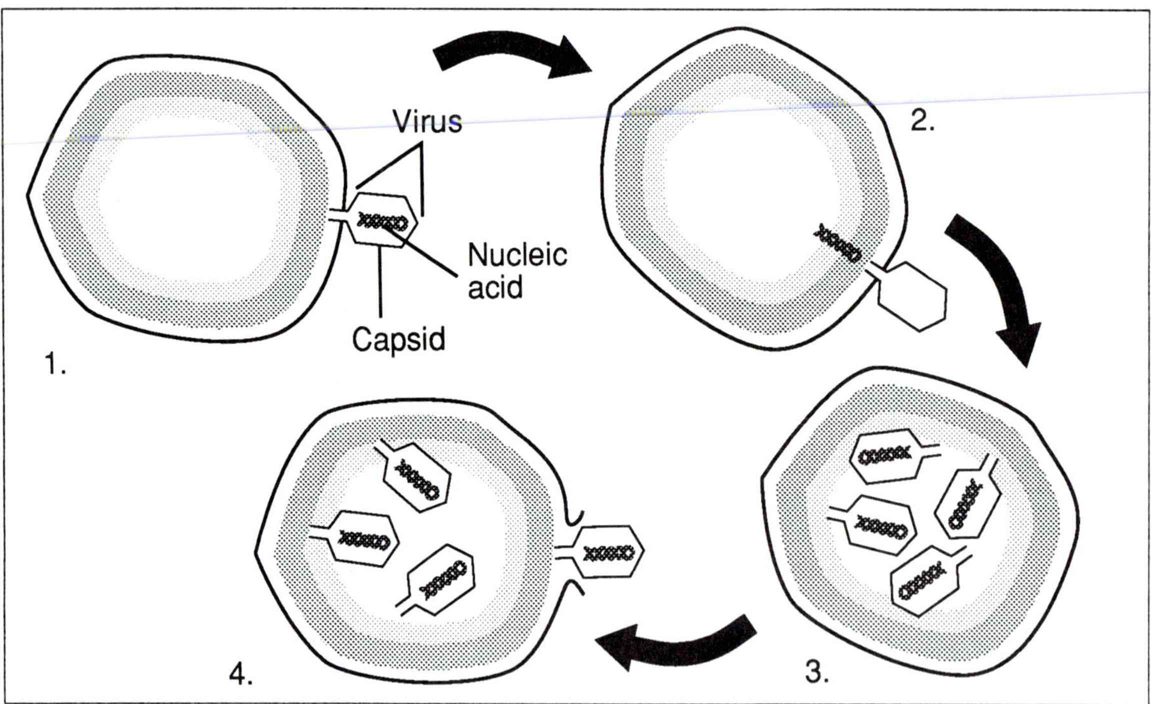

Figure C

FILL IN THE BLANK

Complete each statement using a term or terms from the list below. Write your answers in the spaces provided. Some words may be used more than once.

diseases	reproduction	cell
shapes	infect	capsid
nucleic acid	animal	smaller

1. Scientists classify viruses according to the living things they _______________.
2. A virus is just a pieces of _______________ covered by protein.
3. Some viruses have very unusual _______________.
4. The outer coat of a virus is called a _______________.
5. Capsids give viruses their _______________.
6. The three main groups of viruses are bacterial, plant and _______________ viruses.
7. Viruses are much _______________ than bacteria.
8. A virus does not carry out any of the life processes except _______________.

   However, it can only reproduce inside another living _______________.
9. A virus has no _______________ parts.
10. Viruses cause many plant and animal _______________.

TRUE OR FALSE

In the space provided, write "true" if the sentence is true. Write "false" if the sentence is false.

__________ 1. The flu is caused by a virus.

__________ 2. The capsid makes up most of a virus.

__________ 3. All viruses are round.

__________ 4. When viruses reproduce, the capsid enters a cell.

__________ 5. The outer coat of a virus is made up of protein

__________ 6. The nucleic acid gives a virus it's shape.

__________ 7. Viruses do not ingest or digest food.

__________ 8. Scientists first learned about how viruses reproduce by studying animal viruses.

MORE ABOUT VIRAL REPRODUCTION

Match each statement to the stages showing how viruses reproduce. Write the letter of each statement below the correct stage.

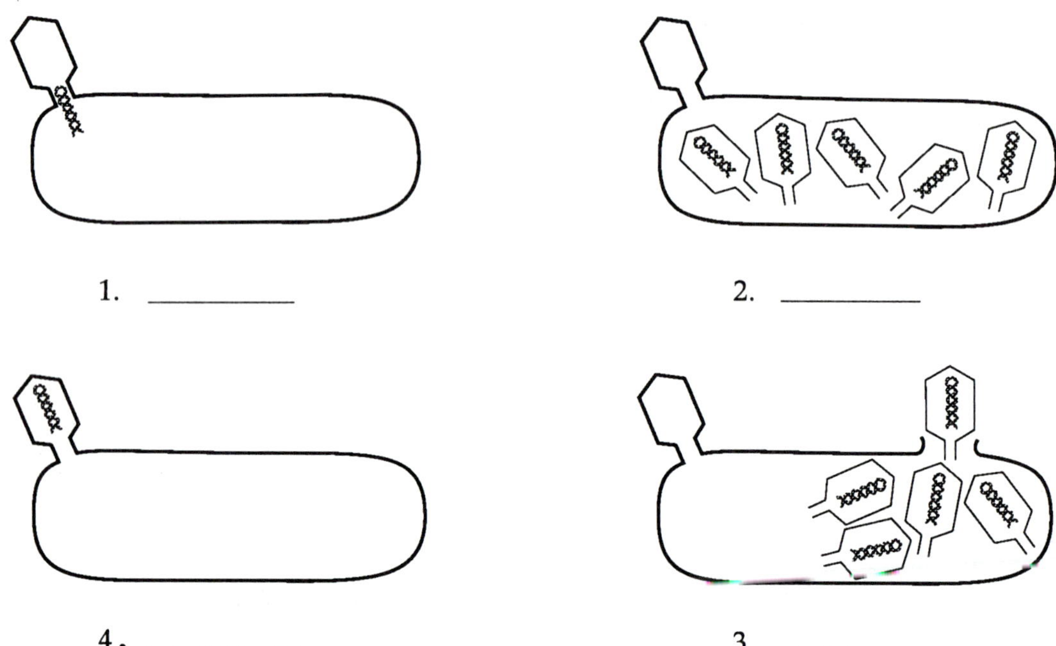

Figure D

a. Bacterial virus attaches itself to the host cell
b. Virus injects its nucleic acid into the cell.
c. Nucleic acid of virus directs the cell to make new viral nucleic acid and capsids.
d. New viruses burst out of the host cell.

REACHING OUT

Do you think viral infections are hard to treat? Explain why or why not.

____

____

____

What are infectious diseases?

16

AIDS: viral disease that attacks a person immune system

contagious [kuhn-TAY-jus] **disease**: infectious disease that can be transmitted from person to person

immune system: body system made up of cells and tissues that help a person fight disease

infectious [in-FEK-shus] **disease**: disease caused when a virus (or germs) enter the body

LESSON 16 | What are infectious diseases?

Disease is a great enemy of living things. A disease interferes with the normal functions of an organism.

Diseases injure or kill millions of people each year. Diseases also infect plants and other animals. They destroy crops. They kill animals such as cattle, and chickens.

Some diseases are caused by germs that enter the body. The germs may be bacteria, viruses, or other microscopic organisms. These diseases are called **infectious** [in-FEK-shus] **diseases**. The "flu" is an example of an infectious disease. As you learned in Lesson 16, it is caused by a virus.

Disease symptoms develop when microbes destroy cells. Most disease-causing bacteria produce poisons called toxins. These toxins kill the cells. Some microbes live in cells. They multiply so fast that the cells die.

Some infectious diseases can be spread from one person to another. These kinds of infectious diseases are **contagious** [kuhn-TAY-jus] **diseases**. Have you ever heard someone with a cold say, "Don't come close. I might be contagious"? The common cold is a contagious disease.

Now let us examine some of the ways diseases are spread.

- Some diseases are spread through the air. When an infected person coughs or sneezes, germs are sprayed into the air.
- Many diseases are spread by taking in food or water that contains germs.
- Some are spread by contact with objects that have germs.
- The bite of an insect spreads certain diseases.
- Some diseases are spread by direct contact with an infected person.

SOME COMMON INFECTIOUS DISEASES OF HUMANS

The chart below lists several infectious diseases of humans. Study the chart. Then answer the questions on the next page.

DISEASE	CAUSED BY	SYMPTOMS
Chicken pox	Virus	fever, headache, skin rashes, that form crusts
Measles	Virus	fever, rash, sensitivity to light, cough, body aches
Botulism [BAHCH-uh-lizm]	Bacteria	double vision, abdominal pain, heart and lung paralysis
Malaria	Protozoa	fever, chills
Strep Throat	Bacteria	fever, sore throat
Mumps	Virus	fever, chills, headache, swollen neck and throat glands
Influenza [in-floo-EN-zuh] (flu)	Virus	fever, chills, body aches, [and possibly a sore throat and cough]
Athlete's foot	Fungus	itchy skin
Polio	Virus	fever, sore throat, stiff back, muscle pain, paralysis
Tetanus	Bacteria	tightening of muscles

1. How many of these common diseases have you had? ______________________

2. Which diseases have you had? ______________________

3. a) What are the symptoms of malaria? ______________________

____

   b) What causes malaria? ______________________

4. Which diseases listed in the chart are caused by bacteria? ______________________

____

5. Which of the diseases are caused by a virus? ______________________

____

MATCHING

Match the disease listed in Column A to its symptoms in Column B

		Column A		Column B
________	1.	polio	a)	fever, chills, swollen neck and throat glands
________	2.	chicken pox	b)	fever, headache, skin rashes that form crusts
________	3.	athlete's foot	c)	fever, sore throat, stiff back, muscle pain, paralysis
________	4.	tetanus	d)	tightening of muscles
________	5.	mumps	e)	itchy skin

ANIMAL DISEASES

Farm animals like cattle, hogs, and sheep, are called livestock.

Animal diseases kill more than two billion dollars worth of livestock each year in the United States alone.

One of the worst livestock diseases is hoof-and-mouth disease. It is caused by a virus and it spreads very rapidly. Many of the infected animals die.

A farmer may have to kill all the animals that are near an infected animal to prevent a epidemic. An epidemic is the spread of a disease to many organisms in an area at the same time.

Figure A

PLANT DISEASES

At one time, the most important food crop in Ireland was the potato.

During the 1840s, a fungus disease destroyed the potato crop in Ireland. Between 1845 and 1847, nearly 750,000 people died of starvation. Hundreds of thousands of others fled the country in search of food and a new life. Many of these people came to the United States.

Figure B

FILL IN THE BLANK

Complete each statement using a term or terms from the list below. Write your answers in the spaces provided.

contagious	toxins	coughs
spread	virus	infectious
insect	hoof-and-mouth	epidemic
sneezes	fungus	

1. Contagious diseases can be ______________ from one person to another.
2. One of the worst livestock diseases is ________________ disease.
3. Diseases caused by germs are called ______________ diseases.
4. The bite of an ______________ spreads some diseases.
5. The spread of a disease to many organisms in an area is called an ____________ .
6. Most disease-causing bacteria produce ______________ .
7. The potato famine of Ireland in the 1840s was caused by a ______________ .
8. The "flu" is caused by a ____________ .
9. When an infected person____________ or ____________ germs are sprayed into the air.
10. The common cold is a ______________ disease.

TRUE OR FALSE

In the space provided, write "true" if the sentence is true. Write "false" if the sentence is false.

________ 1. The common cold is not a contagious disease.

________ 2. Athlete's foot is caused by bacteria.

________ 3. Diseases injure or kill millions of people each year.

________ 4. Infectious diseases affect only animals.

________ 5. Germs may be bacteria, viruses, protozoans, or fungi.

________ 6. All infectious diseases are caused by viruses.

________ 7. Hoof-and-mouth disease is one of the worst human diseases.

________ 8. Malaria is an infectious disease.

________ 9. Many diseases are spread by taking in food or water that contains germs.

________ 10. Covering your mouth when you cough helps prevent the spread of germs.

AIDS

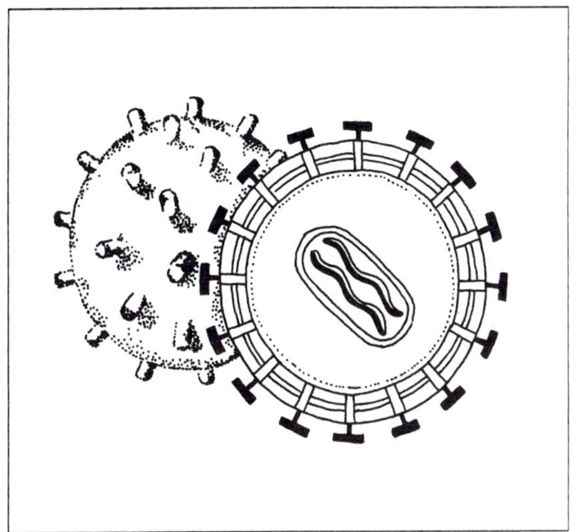

Figure C *HIV virus*

You know that viruses cause many diseases. One particular virus called the HIV virus attacks a person's **immune system**. Your immune system is made up of cells and tissues that fight disease.

The disease caused by the HIV virus is called Acquired Immune Deficiency Syndrome, or **AIDS**.

Because the HIV virus attacks the immune system, a person with AIDS loses the ability to fight disease. The person gets diseases that most healthy people can fight off.

HOW IS AIDS SPREAD?

People with AIDS have the HIV virus in their blood and body fluids. In order to be infected with the HIV virus, you must exchange bodily fluids with an infected person.

The HIV virus can enter the bloodstream by sexual contact with someone who has AIDS. It can also be spread by intravenous drug users who use contaminated needles. A third way the HIV virus enters the bloodstream is through a blood transfusion of infected blood. However, most blood in the United States is tested for the HIV virus.

AIDS TREATMENT

There is no known cure for AIDS at this time. It is a fatal, or deadly, disease.

Scientists are working on ways to treat AIDS patients and make their immune systems stronger. They are also working on AIDS vaccine.

WAYS OF AIDS INFECTION

Place a check mark beside each statement that describes a way that a person can become infected with the AIDS virus.

__________ **1.** from a dog bite

__________ **2.** exchange of body fluids with an infected person

__________ **3.** sexual contact with an infected person

__________ **4.** from a mosquito bite

__________ **5.** through casual contact with an infected person

__________ **6.** by a contaminated needle

Complete the following

1. What is AIDS? ______________________________

2. What do the letters in the word "AIDS" stand for? ____________________

____

3. What is the name of the virus that causes AIDS? ____________________

4. What is the immune system? ______________________________

____

5. Why are diseases that a healthy person can fight off sometimes fatal to a person with AIDS? ______________________________

____

What are noninfectious diseases?

17

noninfectious diseases: diseases that are not caused by germs and not spread from person to person

LESSON 17 What are noninfectious diseases?

In Lesson 16, you learned that infectious diseases are caused by germs. But what about other diseases such as heart disease? These are diseases too. However, they are not caused by germs. They are called **noninfectious diseases.**

A noninfectious disease is not spread from person to person. Some noninfectious diseases last for a long time or keep coming back. These kinds of diseases are called chronic illnesses. Cancer is one example of a chronic illness.

There are many groups of noninfectious diseases. Some of the major noninfectious diseases are identified below.

HEART DISEASE is the leading cause of death in the United States. Heart disease develops when the normal flow of blood through the heart or body is stopped in some way. Some common forms of heart disease are heart attacks, strokes, and high blood pressure.

CANCER occurs when certain cells in the body grow without control. The cancer cells destroy normal tissue. If left untreated, most kinds of cancer cause death. However, many forms of cancer can be treated if they are caught early enough.

ARTHRITIS is a general term for conditions that affect the joints. Arthritis causes pain and swelling in many joints of the body. You may think that arthritis affects mostly older people. Some forms do. However, others strike people of all ages.

MORE ABOUT DISEASE

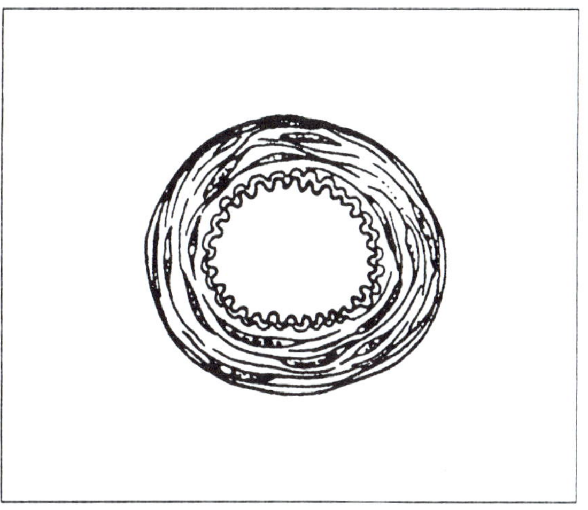

Figure A *Healthy artery*

In one kind of heart disease. fatty substances build up. They build up on the walls of the arteries. One of these fatty substances is cholesterol [kuh-LES-tuh-rohl]. Cholesterol is a fatty substance found in animal products.

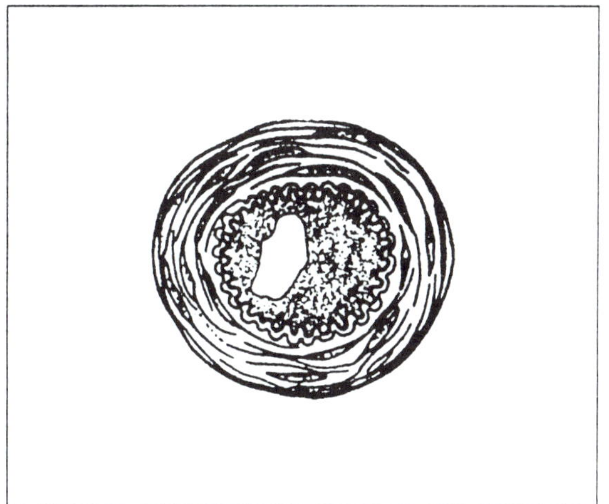

Figure B *Diseased artery*

As fat builds up in an artery, the artery becomes more narrow. This makes the heart have to work harder. The heart must work harder to pump blood through narrow arteries.

HEART ATTACKS AND STROKES

Sometimes the arteries leading to the heart are blocked. This prevents food and oxygen from reaching the heart. Then the heart cannot do its work. This is called a heart attack.

If the arteries to the brain are blocked, food and oxygen cannot reach the brain, this is called a stroke.

CAN YOU PREVENT HEART DISEASE?

Do you think heart disease can be prevented? Scientists have found that there are several things that increase a person's chance of getting heart disease. Some of these things cannot be changed. However, others can be controlled.

Look at the chart below. It shows the major factors that lead to heart disease. Then answer the questions below the chart.

FACTORS CONTRIBUTING TO HEART DISEASE

• age (risk increases with age)	• high blood pressure
• family history (runs in families)	• obesity
• gender (men are at greater risk than women)	• physical inactivity
• smoking	• high cholesterol levels

1. Which factors do you think cannot be controlled? ____________________

____

2. Which factors may be controlled? ____________________

____

TRUE OR FALSE

In the space provided, write "true" if the sentence is true. Write "false" if the sentence is false.

________ **1.** The heart must work harder to pump blood through narrow arteries.

________ **2.** Cholesterol is a fatty substance found in plant products.

________ **3.** There are several risk factors for heart disease.

________ **4.** When arteries to the heart are blocked, a stroke occurs.

________ **5.** Heart attacks and strokes are the only forms of heart disease.

________ **6.** Smoking increases your risk for heart disease.

________ **7.** Arteries to the heart bring it food and oxygen.

________ **8.** The risk of heart disease increases with age.

________ **9.** You can control all the risk factors for heart disease.

________ **10.** Women have a greater risk of heart disease than men.

MORE ABOUT CANCER

Cells in the body usually divide and grow in an orderly manner. Sometimes growth goes wild. Cells grow out of control. The cells form a mass, or lump, called a tumor [TOO-mur].

There are two kinds of tumors:

BENIGN [bi-NYN] TUMORS only grow in one place in the body. A benign tumor does not spread to other places. It is usually not a serious problem.

MALIGNANT [muh-LIG-nunt] TUMORS spread to other places in the body. As a malignant tumor spreads, it harms the body. If its growth is not stopped, a person with a malignant tumor may die. Cancer is the disease a person with a malignant tumor has.

Scientists are not sure what causes all types of cancer. But, they do know that certain things cause cancer or increase a person's chance of getting cancer. Some of these things are smoking, X rays, and too much sunlight.

EARLY SIGNS OF CANCER

The earlier cancer is detected, the more likely a person is to survive. The chart below list the seven warning signs of cancer. A person with any of these signs, should see a doctor immediately.

1. A sore that does not heal
2. Unusual bleeding
3. A lump in the breast or other area beneath the skin
4. Constant indigestion or trouble swallowing
5. A nagging cough
6. A change in size, shape or color of a wart or mole
7. A change in bowel or bladder habits

MATCHING

Match each term in Column A with its description in column B. Write the correct letter in the space provided.

	Column A	Column B
______	**1.** cancer	**a)** harmless mass of cells
______	**2.** benign tumor	**b)** any mass or lump of cells
______	**3.** tumor	**c)** rapid, uncontrolled growth of cells
______	**4.** malignant tumor	**d)** harmful mass of cells that can spread throughout the body
______	**5.** sunlight	**e)** possible cause of skin cancer

WARNING SIGNS OF CANCER

Place a check mark beside each statement that describes one of the seven warning signs of cancer.

________	1. unusual bleeding	________	6. change in size of a mole
________	2. thirst	________	7. changes in color of a mole
________	3. nagging cough	________	8. lump beneath the skin
________	4. sore that does not heal	________	9. sleeplessness
________	5. constant hunger	________	10. constant indigestion

Study the illustrations. Place a check mark below each illustration that shows a possible cause of cancer.

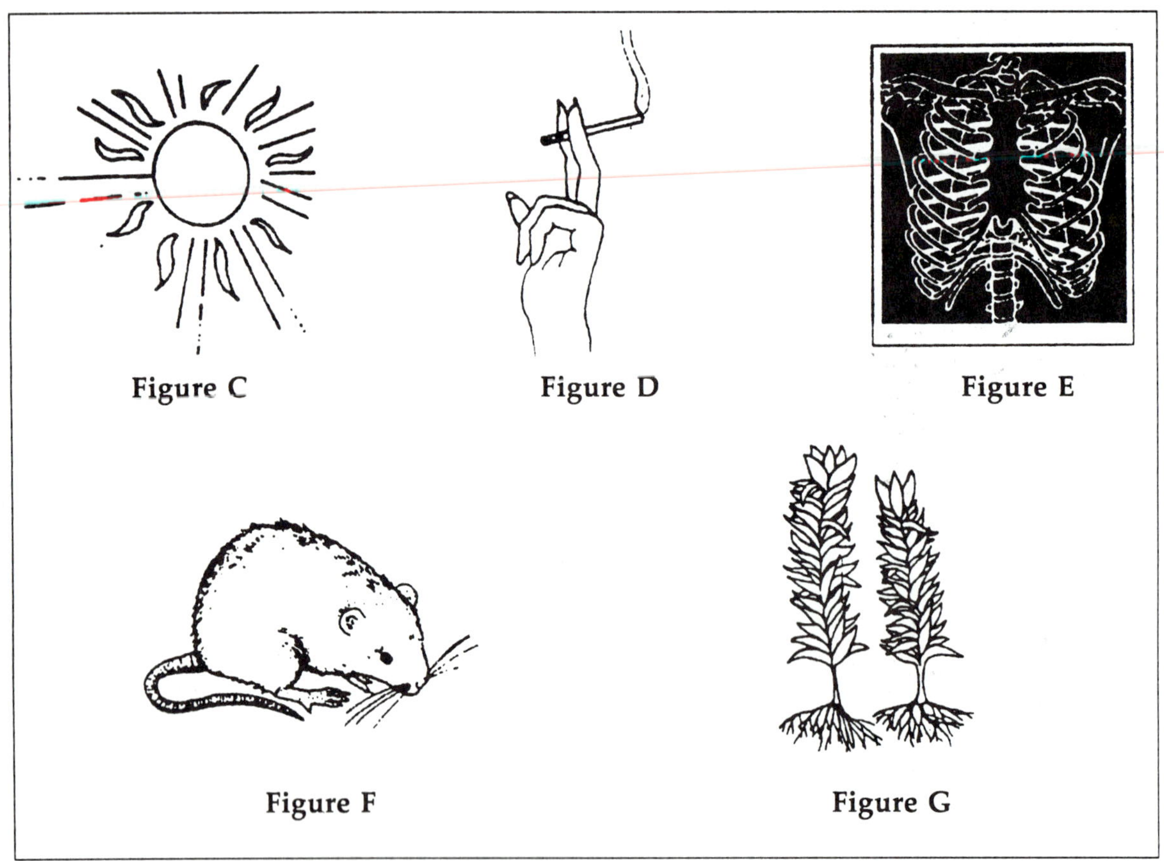

Figure C

Figure D

Figure E

Figure F

Figure G

SOME OTHER NONINFECTIOUS DISEASES

Heart disease, cancer and arthritis are only three of the many noninfectious diseases. Other groups of noninfectious diseases are described below.

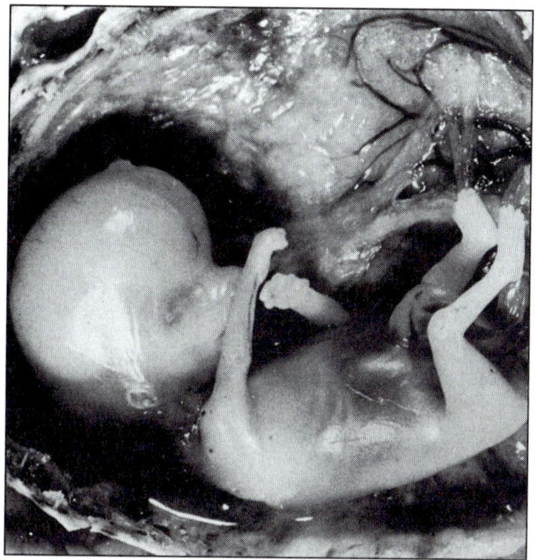

Figure H

Some diseases and disorders, are present at birth. They include heart, lung, and eye problems, blood disorders, hemophilia, bone deformities, and mental retardation.

Some congenital diseases are passed on by genes. They are inherited. However, some others are caused by an unhealthy environment before birth. For example, babies can be born with many problems if their parents take drugs.

NUTRITIONAL DISEASES

Other types of diseases are caused by an improper diet. These are called nutritional diseases. The table below lists some nutritional diseases.

NUTRITIONAL DISEASES		
DISEASE	**SYMPTOMS**	**CAUSED BY A DEFICIENCY OF**
Anemia	lack of energy	Vitamins B_6, B_{12}, or iron
Scurvy	sore gums	Vitamin C
Rickets	soft bones and teeth	Vitamin D; Calcium
night blindness	difficulty seeing in dark	Vitamin A
goiter	swollen thyroid gland	Iodine

FILL IN THE BLANK

Complete each statement using a term or terms from the list below. Write your answers in the spaces provided.

fatty	joints	tumor
brain	genes	heart
cells	birth	vitamin C
narrow		

1. Arthritis is a general term for conditions that affect the _______________ .
2. A stroke occurs when arteries to the _______________ are blocked.
3. A benign _______________ is usually not a serious problem.
4. The leading cause of death in the United States is _______________ disease.
5. Some congenital diseases are passed on by _______________ .
6. Congenital diseases are present at _______________ .
7. Cholesterol is a _______________ substance.
8. The heart must work harder to pump blood through _______________ arteries.
9. Scurvy is caused by lack of _______________ in the diet.
10. Cancer occurs when _______________ grow and divide without control.

REACHING OUT

Many foods advertise that they have no cholesterol or are low in cholesterol. Why do you think companies use this as a selling point? ________________________

____

____

____

____

____

Figure I

How does the body protect itself from disease?

18

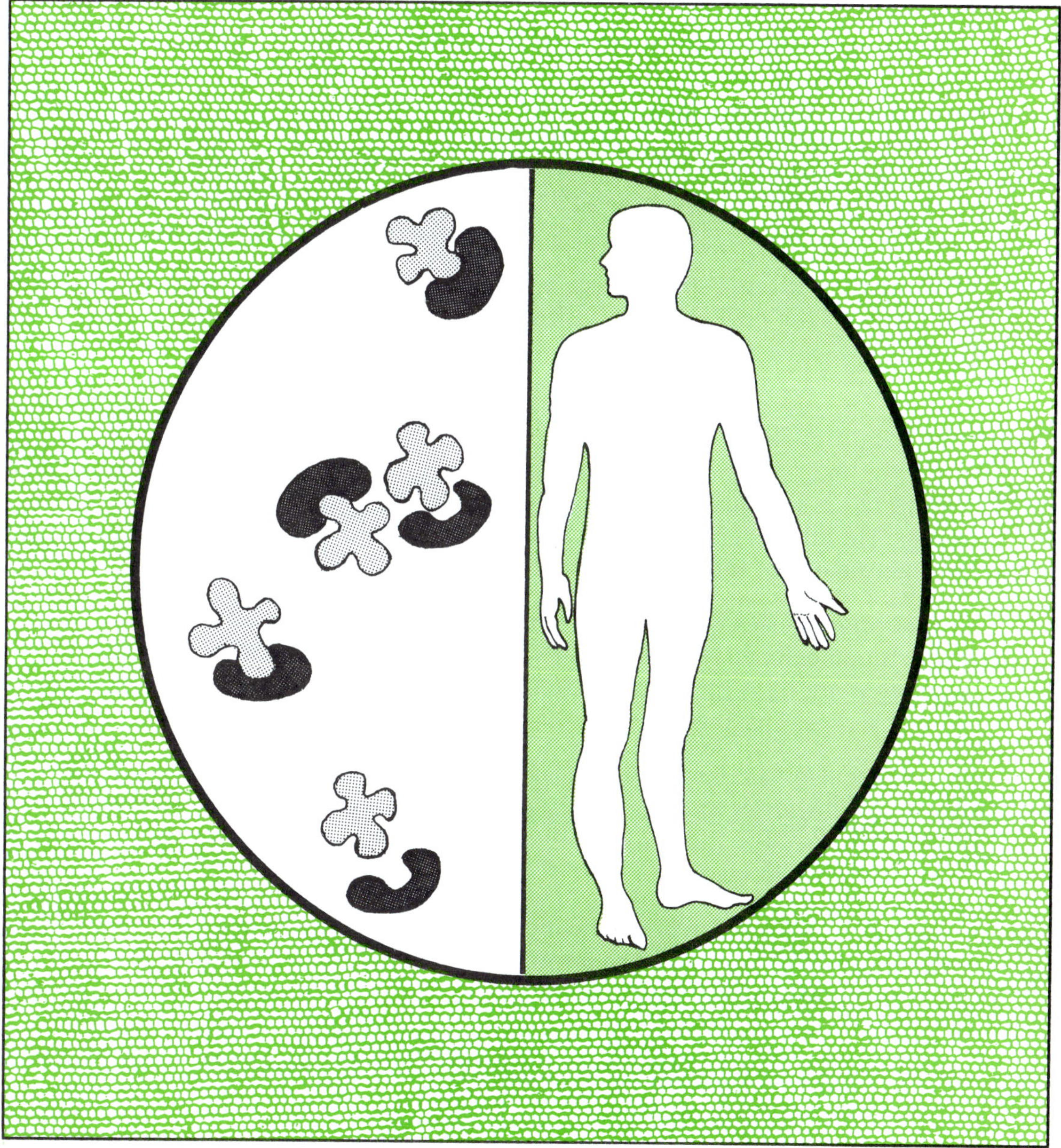

antibodies [AN-ti-bahd-eez]: proteins made by the body that destroy germs
cilia [SIL-ee-uh]: tiny hairlike structures
immunity [im-MYOON-i-tee]: resistance to a certain disease
mucus [MYOU-kus]: sticky substance that traps germs
white blood cells: cells that protect the body against disease

LESSON 18 How does the body protect itself from disease?

Your body is under constant attack from viruses. bacteria, and other germs. However, your body can usually protect itself from disease. It has defenses against germs.

Your skin is your body's first line of defense. The skin is a waterproof, germ-proof barrier that covers your body. The skin acts like a wall to keep out germs.

Your mouth and nose are two places where germs can enter the body. The inside of the nose is lined with small hairs and sticky liquid called **mucus.** The hairs filter out dust and pollen from the air. The mucus traps germs (usually bacteria) as well as dust and pollen

Your windpipe, like the nose, is lined with mucus. It also is lined with very tiny (microscopic) hairs called **cilia** [SIL-ee-uh]. Cilia are always beating in an outward direction. The mucus traps many harmful substances. The cilia sweep them outward. Coughing and sneezing also help force germs out of the body.

Now suppose germs do get by the body's first defenses. What happens? **White blood cells** go to work. It is the job of white blood cells to destroy germs that are harmful to the body. Special white blood cells surround germs by digesting them.

Your body also has one more line of defense. The body is able to make chemical substances that destroy germs. These substances are called **antibodies** [AN-ti-bahd-eez]. Antibodies clump together with germs and destroy them.

In Lesson 17, you learned that the immune system is made up of tissues and cells that fight disease. The immune system is in charge of recognizing germs and making antibodies.

KEEP THEM OUT!

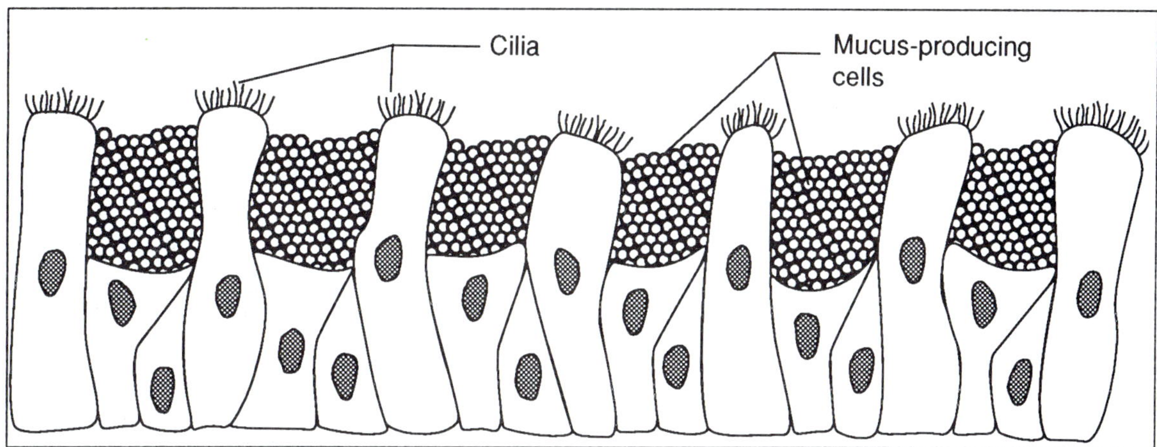

Figure A *The cilia and mucus in the nose are part of the body's first line of defense.*

1. The nose is lined with small __________ and sticky liquid called__________.
2. The hairs and mucus filter and trap __________, __________, and __________.
3. Trapped dust and pollen "tickle" our noses. This makes us __________.
4. How do sneezing and coughing help fight disease? __________
5. Why should you always "cover" a sneeze or cough? __________

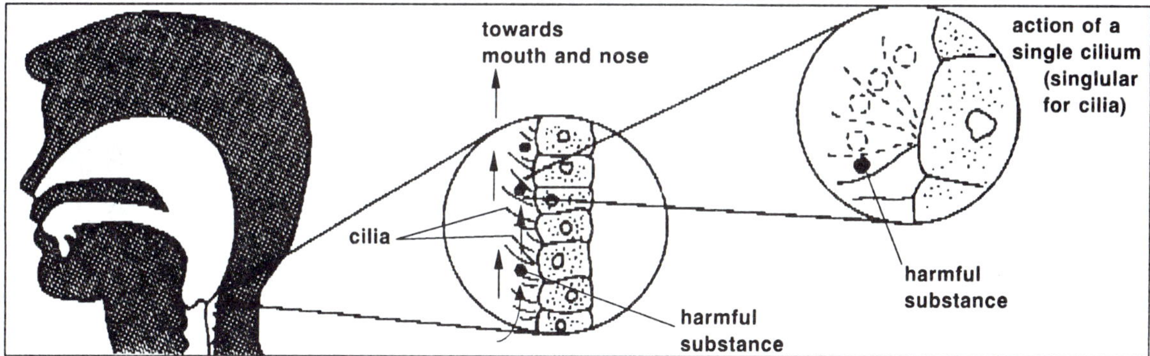

Figure B

6. Harmful substances that reach the windpipe are trapped by __________.
7. They are swept outward by microscopic hairs called __________.
8. Cilia in the windpipe are always moving towards __________.
the lungs, the mouth and nose

BODY DEFENSES

Study the pictures below. Then answer the questions.

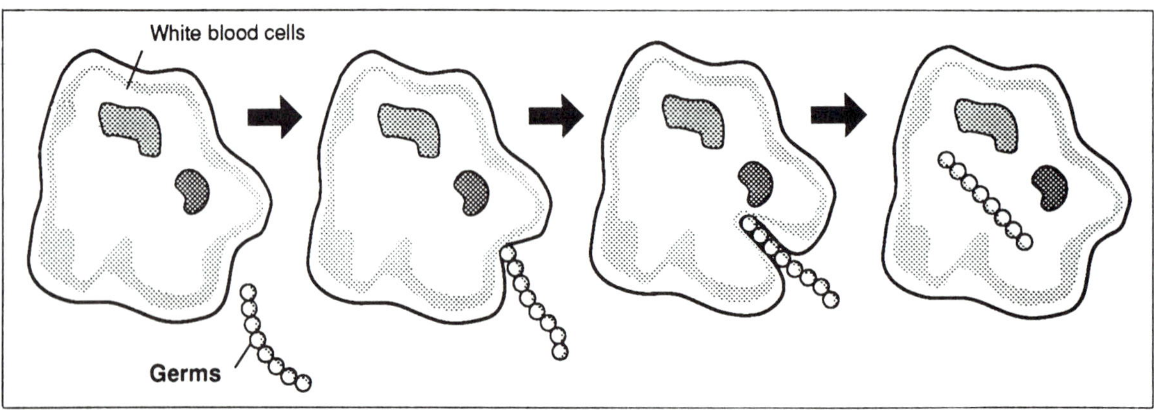

Figure C

1. What kind of blood cells fight germs in the body? ______________________

2. What is happening in Figure C? ______________________

____

____

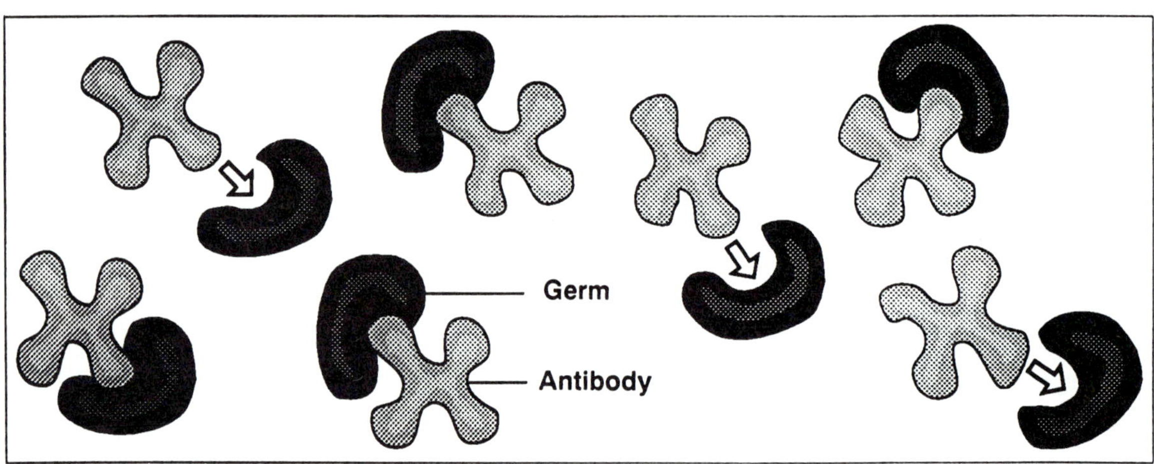

Figure D

3. What chemical substances does the body make to fight germs? ______________________

4. What is happening in Figure D? ______________________

____

5. What body system is in charge of making antibodies? ______________________

FILL IN THE BLANK

Complete each statement using a term or terms from the list below. Write your answers in the spaces provided. Some words may be used more than once.

sticky	immune system	defenses
outward	antibodies	germs
filter	skin	surround

1. Your body has ______________ against disease.
2. The immune system produces ______________ .
3. Cilia are always beating in an ______________ direction.
4. The ______________ acts like a wall to keep out germs.
5. White blood cells destroy ______________ that enter the body.
6. Cells and tissues that fight disease make up the ______________ .
7. Hairs in the nose ______________ air.
8. Some white blood cells ______________ germs to destroy them.
9. Chemical substances called ______________ clump together with germs and destroy them.
10. Mucus is a ______________ liquid.

COMPLETE THE TABLE

Complete the table by describing how each part of the body's defense systems helps to protect the body from harmful germs.

Body Defenses Against Disease		
	Defense	**How It Works**
1.	Skin	
2.	Nose	
3.	cilia and Mucus	
4.	White Blood Cells	
5.	Antibodies	

MORE ABOUT THE IMMUNE SYSTEM

Antibodies destroy germs. After the germs are destroyed, many of the antibodies remain. If the same kind of germs enter the body again, the antibodies are "ready and waiting". They destroy the germs before they can do any harm. The body has become resistant.

Resistance to a certain disease is called **immunity** [im-MYOON-i-tee].

There are two kinds of immunity—natural immunity and acquired [uh-KWY-urd] immunity.

- Natural immunity is immunity that you are born with. It is your body's natural defense against disease.
- Acquired immunity is immunity that you get, or develop during your life.

There are several ways you can acquire, or get immunity.

- You can be given a shot of antibodies against a certain disease.
- Developing babies get antibodies from their mothers.
- Once you have had some diseases, your body keeps making antibodies against that disease. Did you ever have chicken pox? if you have, you now have immunity against the chicken pox.
- You can get a vaccine.

Vaccinations are helpful in preventing specific diseases such as polio and the measles. A vaccine is made up of specific dead or weakened disease-causing microbes. However, a vaccine does not cause you to get the disease.

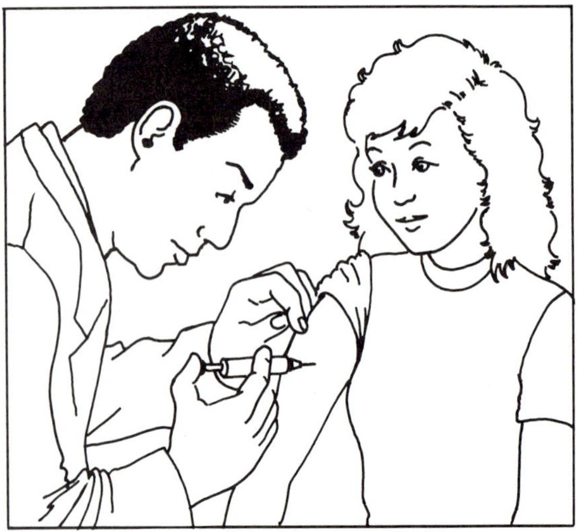

Figure E

How does a vaccine work? The vaccine enters the body by injection, through a scratch or by swallowing. It signals the body to make antibodies.

A vaccinated individual becomes resistant to a specific disease. But a "booster" shot may be required, after a period of time, to keep the immunity.

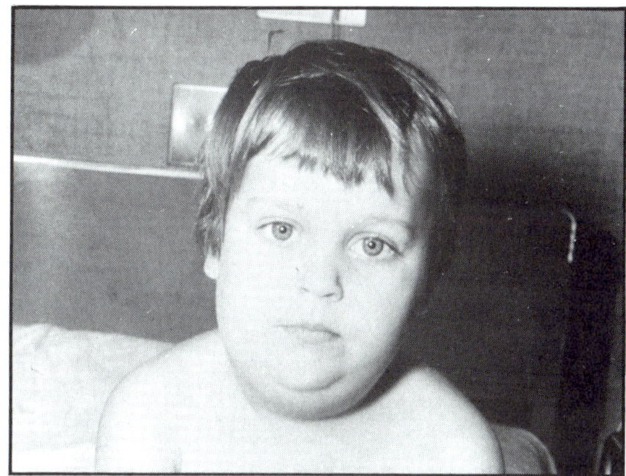

Figure F

The mumps is an infection of the salivary glands. Did you ever have the mumps?

At one time many children had the mumps. Now fewer children have this infection because they have been given a vaccine against it.

THE SEARCH GOES ON

The search to develop new vaccines never stops. Special effort is being made to develop vaccines against cancer and AIDS.

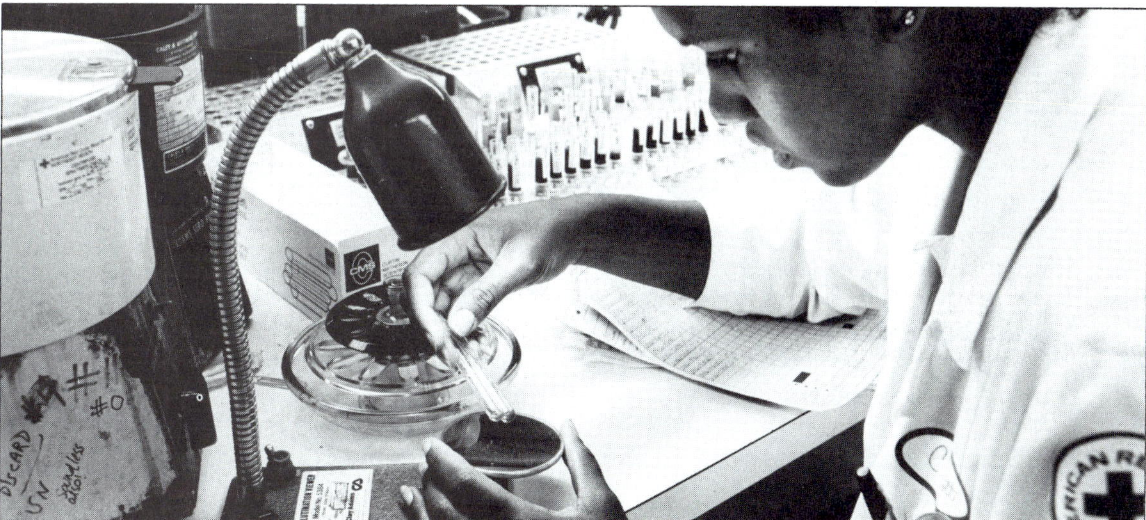

Figure G

TRUE OR FALSE

In the space provided, write "true" if the sentence is true. Write "false" if the sentence is false.

_________ **1.** Acquired immunity is immunity that you are born with.

_________ **2.** Vaccines are helpful in preventing polio and the measles.

_________ **3.** Resistance to a certain disease is called immunity.

_________ **4.** Being given a shot of antibodies is one way to acquire immunity.

_________ **5.** There are vaccines for every disease.

_________ **6.** Vaccines are only given by injection.

_________ **7.** A vaccine causes you to get a disease.

_________ **8.** A booster may be required, to keep immunity against some diseases.

_________ **9.** People are born with natural immunity.

_________ **10.** Developing babies get antibodies from their mothers.

COMPLETE THE TABLE

Complete the table by identifying the kind of immunity that is described in the first column. Place a check mark in the correct column.

	Description	**Natural Immunity**	**Acquired Immunity**
1.	You are injected with a vaccine.		
2.	You are exposed to chicken pox.		
3.	You are born with an immunity.		
4.	You are given a shot of antibodies.		
5.	A developing baby receives an antibody from its mother.		

What are other ways of fighting disease?

19

antibiotic [an-ti-by-AHT-ik]: chemical substances that kill harmful bacteria

LESSON 19 | What are other ways of fighting disease?

Your body has many defenses to protect itself from disease. But sometimes, the body needs help. At these times your doctor may prescribe medicine for you. The doctor may also give you an injection.

Have you ever been prescribed <u>penicillin</u> [pen-uh-SYL-in]? Penicillin was the first **antibiotic** [an-ti-by-AHT-ic] to be discovered. Antibiotics are chemical substances that kill harmful bacteria.

Penicillin was discovered in 1929 by Alexander Fleming. Fleming was an English scientist. He was growing bacteria in a dish and noticed that bacteria did not grow in one part of the dish - the part of the dish where some mold had grown. Fleming guessed that the mold produced a substance that was harmful to bacteria. He was right! The substance was penicillin. Penicillin destroys some bacteria and stops it from reproducing.

There are other antibiotics too. Like penicillin, most are made from molds. However, some come from bacteria and plants.

Antibiotics are <u>not</u> all the same. Each antibiotic can only be used to treat certain diseases. And no antibiotic works against viruses.

Before giving a person an antibiotic, Most doctors ask if the person is allergic to it. That is because antibiotics cause allergic reactions in some people. They may get a fever or rash. In serious cases, a person may not be able to breathe. You should always tell your doctor if you are allergic to any medicines.

PREVENTING DISEASES

The discovery of disease-fighting medicines has been very important in treating disease But the best way to "treat" disease is to prevent it. Here are some ways you can help prevent disease.

Many infectious diseases can be prevented by proper sanitation.

Figure A

Proper canning, pasteurization [PAS-chuh-ruh-ZAY-shun], and refrigeration help prevent infectious diseases caused by food poisoning.

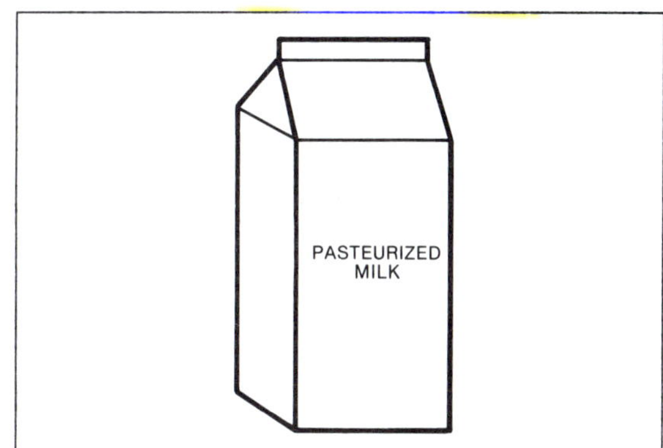

Figure B

Perhaps the best way to avoid disease is to live a healthy life-style. People often get sick when their bodies are run-down. And doctors think that living in a healthy way, lessens your chance of heart disease and some types of cancer.

How can you live a healthy lifestyle?

- Exercise on a regular basis.
- Eat a balanced diet.
- Get enough rest.
- Avoid harmful substances like tobacco.

Figure C

TRUE OR FALSE

In the space provided, write "true" if the sentence is true. Write "false" if the sentence is false.

_________ **1.** Penicillin is made by a mold.

_________ **2.** Antibiotics are all the same.

_________ **3.** Most antibiotics are produced by plants.

_________ **4.** Proper sanitation can help prevent disease.

_________ **5.** Some antibiotics are made by bacteria.

_________ **6.** Penicillin works against viruses.

_________ **7.** An antibiotic is a chemical substance.

_________ **8.** Living a healthy lifestyle has no affect on disease.

_________ **9.** Some people have allergic reactions to penicillin.

_________ **10.** Alexander Fleming was the first person to observe the action of an antibiotic.

WORD SCRAMBLE

Below are several words you have used in this Lesson. Unscramble the words and write your answers in the spaces provided.

1. EMIDCIEN _________________________

2. MDLOS _________________________

3. RATAEBCI _________________________

4. CXEERIES _________________________

5. CENLPILIIN _________________________

What is ecology?

20

biosphere [BY-uh-sfir]: thin zone of the earth that supports all life
community: all the organisms living in a certain area
ecology [ee-KAHL-uh-jee]: study of the relationship between living things and their environment
ecosystem [EE-koh-sis-tum]: all the living things and nonliving parts of an environment
population: all the members of one species that live in the same area

LESSON 20 | What is ecology?

Our planet is huge. It has an area of more than 500 million square kilometers (200 million square miles). Yet life exists only on its surface, and slightly above and below. We call this narrow zone of life the **biosphere** [BY-uh-sfir]. You may know that the term "bio"-means life.

The biosphere is full with all kinds of life. These organisms live in all kinds of environments. Everything that surrounds an organism makes up its environment. Living things are affected by their environment. They can also have an effect on their environments.

The study of the relationship between living things and their environment is called **ecology** [ee-KAHL-uh-jee]. Scientists who study ecology are called ecologists. The living and nonliving parts of a specific environment make up an **ecosystem** [EE-koh-sis-tum]. Some of the nonliving parts of an ecosystem are air, water, sunlight, and soil. Living things need these things to survive.

An ecosystem can be large, like an ocean or jungle. Or it can be small, like a pond or a patch of grass in an empty lot. Even a home aquarium is an ecosystem!

Each ecosystem is made up of one or more **communities**. A community is all the organisms living in a certain area. For example, a pond community may include frogs, fishes, and water lilies.

Members of a community depend upon each other. They also depend upon nonliving things like air, light, and water. The living and nonliving parts of the environment are always interacting. And a change in one part can cause a change in all the parts.

Each community is made up of **populations**. A population is all of the living things of the same species living in the same area. How many students make up the population of your class?

STUDYING ECOSYSTEMS

Figure A shows a lake ecosystem. The parts of this ecosystem are listed below. Next to each part, write living, if it is living. Write nonliving, if the part is not living.

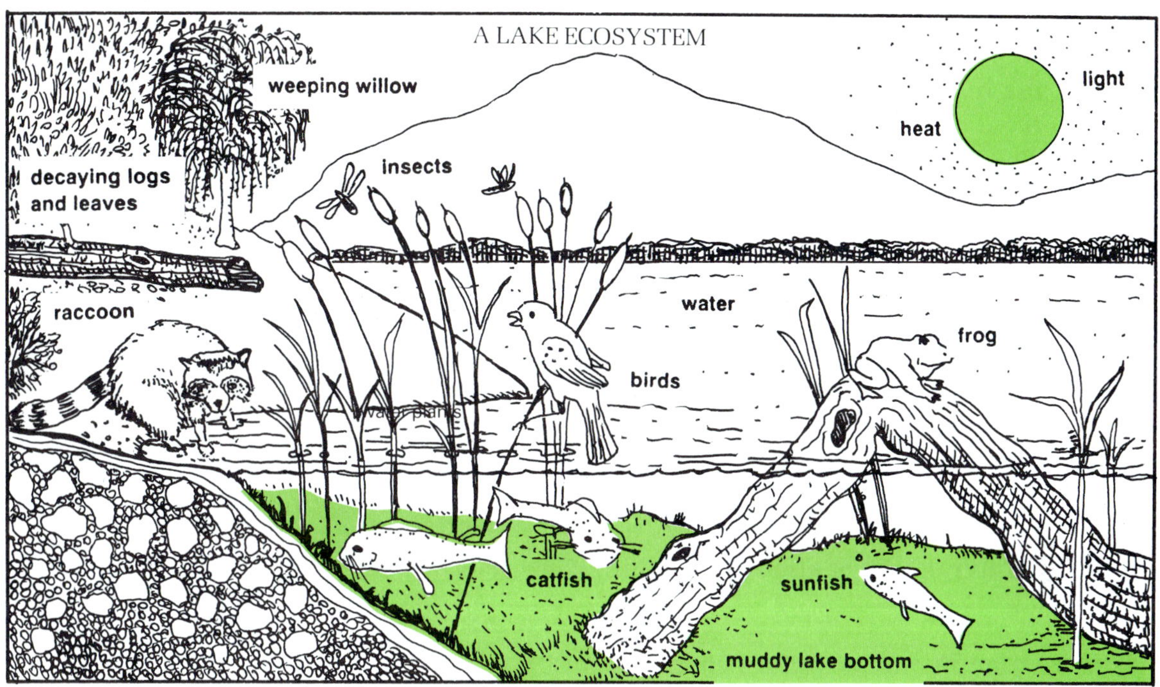

Figure A *A lake ecosystem.*

1. sunlight ______________________
2. catfish ______________________
3. weeping willow tree ______________________
4. raccoon ______________________
5. heat ______________________
6. water ______________________
7. sunfish ______________________
8. water plants ______________________
9. frog ______________________
10. muddy lake bottom ______________________
11. air ______________________
12. insects ______________________
13. bird ______________________
14. bacteria, algae, and other one-celled organisms (not shown, but always present in a lake ecosystem) ______________________
15. Why are the one-celled organisms not shown? ______________________

COMPLETING SENTENCES

Complete the following sentences.

1. An ecosystem is made up of ______________________ things.

2. All the living members of an ecosystem make up __________________ .

3. The region of Earth where life exists is called the __________________ .

4. All of the living and nonliving parts of an organism's surrounding are called its ______________ .

5. Do living things affect nonliving things? ___________ (yes, no)

6. Do nonliving things affect living things? ___________ (yes, no)

7. A change in one part of an environment ___________ (can, cannot) cause a change in another part of the environment.

8. The study of the relationship between organisms and their environment is called ______________ .

REACHING OUT

An aquarium is an ecosystem you may have in your home. A balanced aquarium is a healthy ecosystem. It is one in which all the organisms receive all the things they need to live.

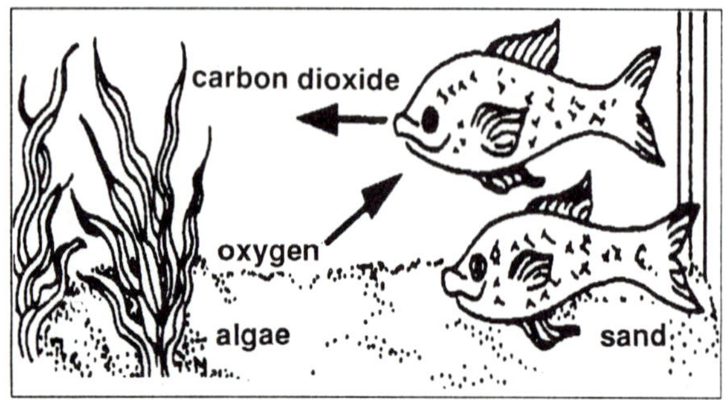

Figure B

What are the living and nonliving parts of an aquarium ecosystem?

living ______________________

nonliving ______________________

____

What are some other characteristics of an ecosystem?

21

consumers [kun-SOO-murs]: organisms that get food by eating other organisms
decomposers [dee-kum-POHZ-ers]: organisms that feed on dead organisms
habitat [HAB-i-tat]: place where an organism lives
niche [NICH]: an organism's role, or job, in its environment
producers: organisms that can make their own food

LESSON 21 | What are some other characteristics of an ecosystem?

If someone asked you where you live, how would you answer? The place where an organism lives is its **habitat** [HAB-i-tat]. A habitat is a special place. It provides all of an organisms's needs, like food and air. It provides an organism with shelter. It also provides a place to reproduce. Sometimes, different species share the same habitat. For example, insects and mushrooms may share the same rotting log. Birds, squirrels, and insects might live in the same tree.

Now suppose someone asked what your role or job in life is. You would probably say that you are a student. Being a student is the job or role that you do where you live. Organisms also have jobs and roles in their communities. The job of a living thing is called its **niche** [NICH].

Living things may have the same habitat but they do not have the same niche. For example, tigers and deer both share a habitat in Asia. But while tigers chase and eat deer—deer eat grasses. They do not have the same role.

Although the tigers and deer in Asia have different roles, they are related by how they get their food. Each ecosystem is made up of different kinds of organisms.

Some are **producers**. Producers can make their own food. On land, the main producers are plants. In lakes and oceans, algae are the main producers.

Others are **consumers** [kun-SOO-murs]. Consumers get food by eating other organisms. Some consumers eat only plants. Others eat meat, or other animals. And some, like you, eat both plants and animals.

Some animals feed upon dead animals. They eat animals that have died or that have been killed by other animals. For example, vultures eat dead animals.

Bacteria break down the wastes or remains of organisms. They are **decomposers** [dee-kum-POHZ-ers]. Decomposers return materials from dead organisms to the soil.

FOOD CHAINS

Living things depend upon each other for food. Every living thing is a link in a food chain. A food chain shows the order in which living things feed upon other living things.

Look at Figure A. It shows a food chain. The arrows in the food chain show the direction that food moves along the chain.

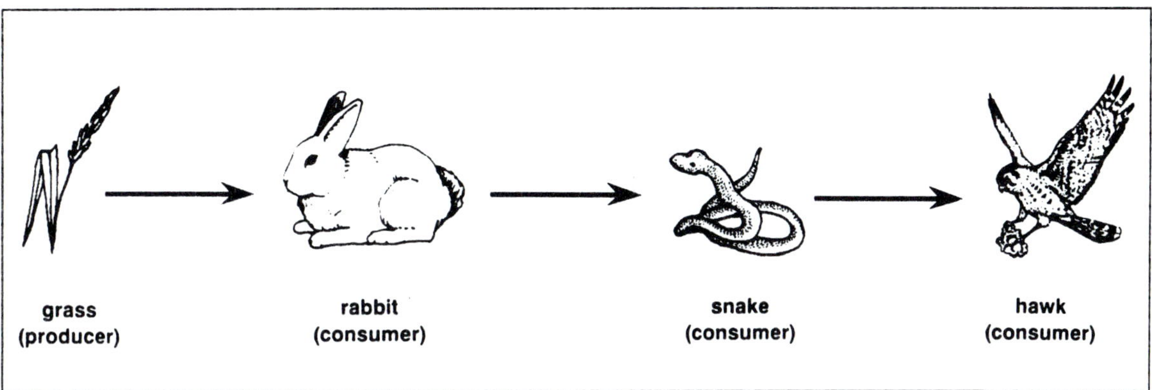

Figure A

Not all organisms eat the same kinds of food. Therefore, there are many different food chains. But, all food chains begin with PRODUCERS.

WHY?

Producers are the only organisms that can make their own food, using energy from the sun.

Why is the sun the source of energy in an ecosystem? ______________________________

____

____

____

FINDING THE MISSING LINKS IN FOOD CHAINS

Six food chains are shown below. One link has been left out of each chain. Identify the organism that is missing. Write your answers in the proper spaces below. Some blank spaces have more than one answer.

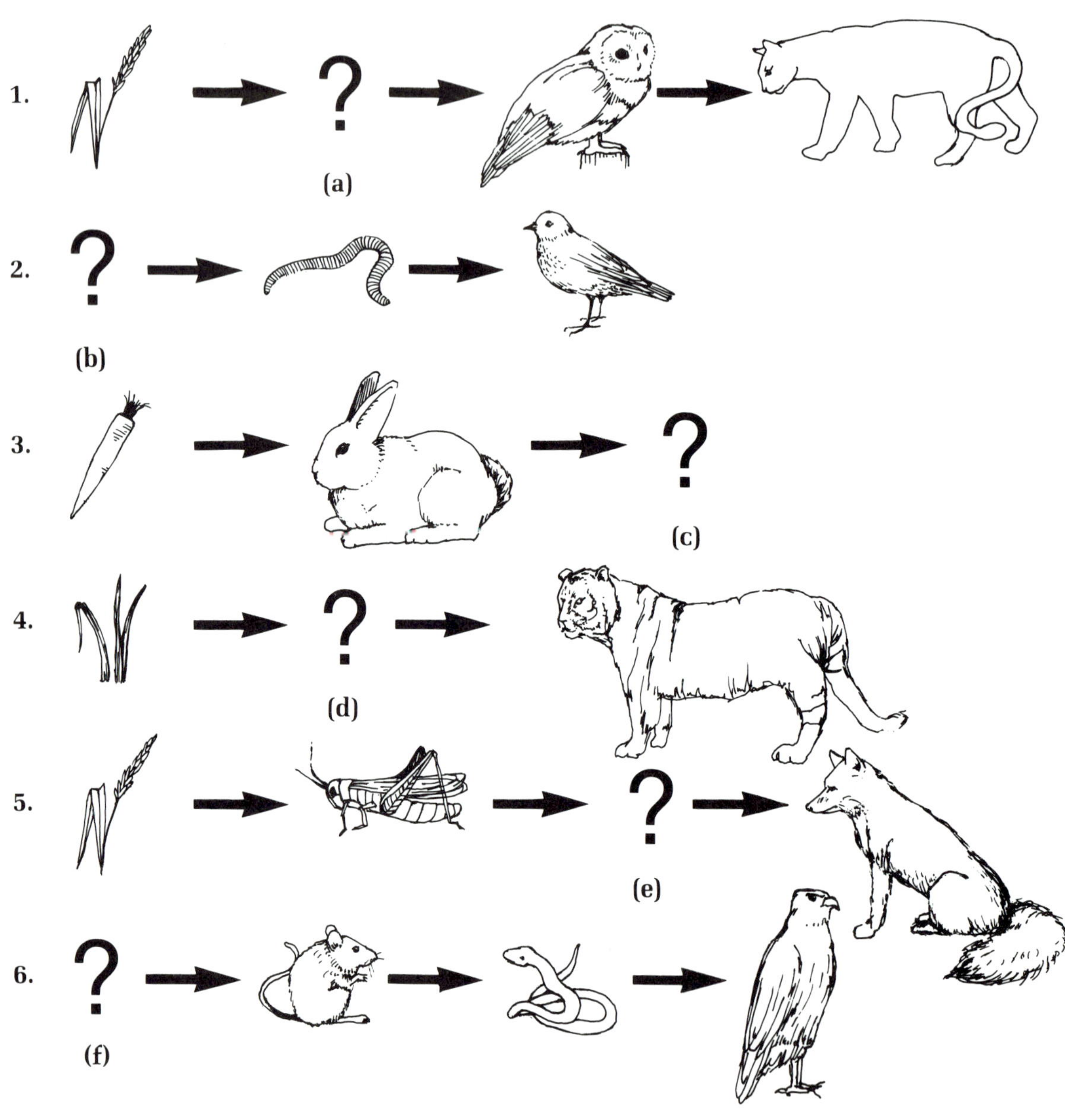

Figure B

1. a. ________________	**4. d.** ________________
2. b. ________________	**5. e.** ________________
3. c. ________________	**6. f.** ________________

FOOD WEBS

You have just learned that food chains show food relationships. However, in nature, many food chains combine and overlap. They form a food web. A food web is a more complete way of showing food relationships. A food web shows how a number of food chains are related.

Look at the food web in Figure C. Then answer the questions.

1. What is the diagram shown called?

   ____

2. What does the diagram show?

   ____

3. What two organisms does a rabbit eat? ______________________________

4. What organisms do wolves eat?

   ____

5. Which organism is the producer?

   ____

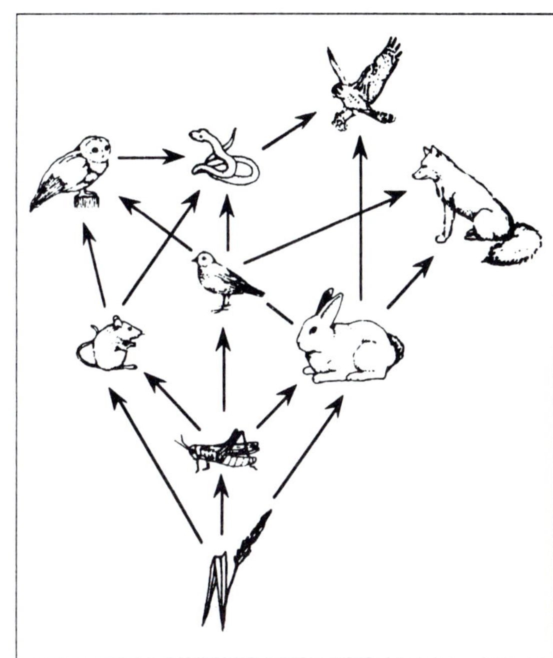

Figure C

MAKE YOUR OWN FOOD CHAIN

In the space provided, draw one of the food chains shown in the diagram above.

COMPLETE THE CHART

*Classify each description as a **habitat** or **niche** by checking the correct column.*

Habitat and Niche			
	Description	**Habitat**	**Niche**
1.	Eaten by fish		
2.	Under rocks		
3.	Hole in a tree		
4.	Eat mice		
5.	Nest on a tree branch		
6.	Eat seeds and fruit		
7.	Log		
8.	Jungle		
9.	Shared by organisms		
10.	Not shared by organisms		

MATCHING

Match each term in Column A with its description in Column B. Write the correct letter in the space provided.

	Column B	**Column B**
________	**1.** plants	**a)** organism that makes its own food.
________	**2.** producer	**b)** animal that feed on other animals
________	**3.** decomposer	**c)** eats dead animals
________	**4.** consumers	**d)** organism that breaks down the wastes or remains of other organisms
________	**5.** vultures	**e)** main producers on land
________	**6.** algae	**f)** main producers in lakes and oceans

COMPLETE THE CHART

Classify each organism listed in the table as a producer, consumer, or decomposer. Place a check mark in the correct column.

	Organism	Producer	Consumer	Decomposer
1.	Seaweed			
2.	Duck			
3.	Hawk			
4.	Ants			
5.	Bacteria			
6.	People			
7.	Rabbits			
8.	Grass			
9.	Apple Tree			
10.	Bees			
11.	Earthworm			
12.	Beetle			

FILL IN THE BLANK

Complete each statement using a term or terms from the list below. Write your answers in the spaces provided.

niche webs food
sun soil

1. A producer can make its own ______________ .
2. The ______________ is the source of energy for an ecosystem.
3. Food chains combine to form food ______________ .
4. The role of an organism is called its ______________ .
5. A decomposer returns materials from dead organisms to the ______________.

CROSSWORD PUZZLE

Use the clues to complete the crossword puzzle.

CLUES

ACROSS

3. organism that gets food by eating other organisms

5. combining and overlapping of many food chains

6. model of the flow of energy through an ecosystem

7. organism that feeds on dead organisms

11. all the members of one species that live in the same area

12. place where an organism lives

13. all the organisms living in a certain area

DOWN

1. an organism's role in its environment

2. organism that makes its own food

4. not dead

8. all the living and nonliving parts of an environment

9. study of the relationship between living things and their environment

10. thin zone of the earth that supports all life.

What are biomes?

22

biomes [BY-ohms]: large region of the earth that has characteristic kinds of organisms

LESSON 22 | What are biomes?

The biosphere is divided into major areas called **biomes** [BY-ohms]. A biome is determined mainly by its climate-like temperature and rainfall. Each biome has a different climate. Climate, in turn, affects the soil. The earth's land areas are divided into six major biomes. They are:

TUNDRA Most of the year, the tundra is bitterly cold and covered with snow and ice. The ground remains permanently frozen. It is called permafrost. Only certain small plants such as mosses and grasses can grow in the tundra. Some animals, like reindeer and foxes, move in during the growing season. But they move out again as the frigid weather approaches. Very few animals live year around in the tundra.

CONIFEROUS FOREST Conifers are cone-bearing trees such as pines and fir trees. Conifers make up the coniferous forest biome. It is an area with a cold climate. Conifers form dense forests. The tree tops block out much of the sunlight. Grasses and smaller trees cannot grow. Only some shrubs, ferns, and mosses thrive. Coniferous forests are "home" for many animals, such as squirrels, moose, birds, and insects.

DECIDUOUS FOREST Deciduous trees such as maples and oaks shed their leaves in the fall. Deciduous forests thrive in moderate climates. Summers may be hot and winters may be cold. But temperatures do not get too hot or too cold for very long time. Deciduous forests receive a good supply of water. They form dense forests. A deciduous forest provides habitats for many kinds of animals.

TROPICAL RAIN FOREST A tropical rain forest is very warm and very moist all the time. It receives plenty of sunlight and rain. This environment is excellent for plant growth and soil development. Plants grow thick and tall. Tropical rain forests are found in areas near the equator. Rain forests support more plant life and animal species than any other biome.

GRASSLANDS The chief plant life in the grassland is grass. Grassland and deciduous forest temperatures are about the same. But grasslands do not receive as much rainfall. Grasslands get enough rain to support grasses—but not trees. Grasslands are excellent for grazing animals. The soil of grass areas is very rich. Wheat and corn are grown here. Grasslands also are "home" for many small, burrowing animals.

DESERT A desert biome is very dry. It receives very little rainfall. Deserts are very hot during the day, but they are cold at night. Desert soil is very dry and poor. Because of this, only a few kinds of plants grow in the desert. And, very few animals can survive in the desert.

MORE ABOUT BIOMES

The map below shows the major land biomes of the earth.

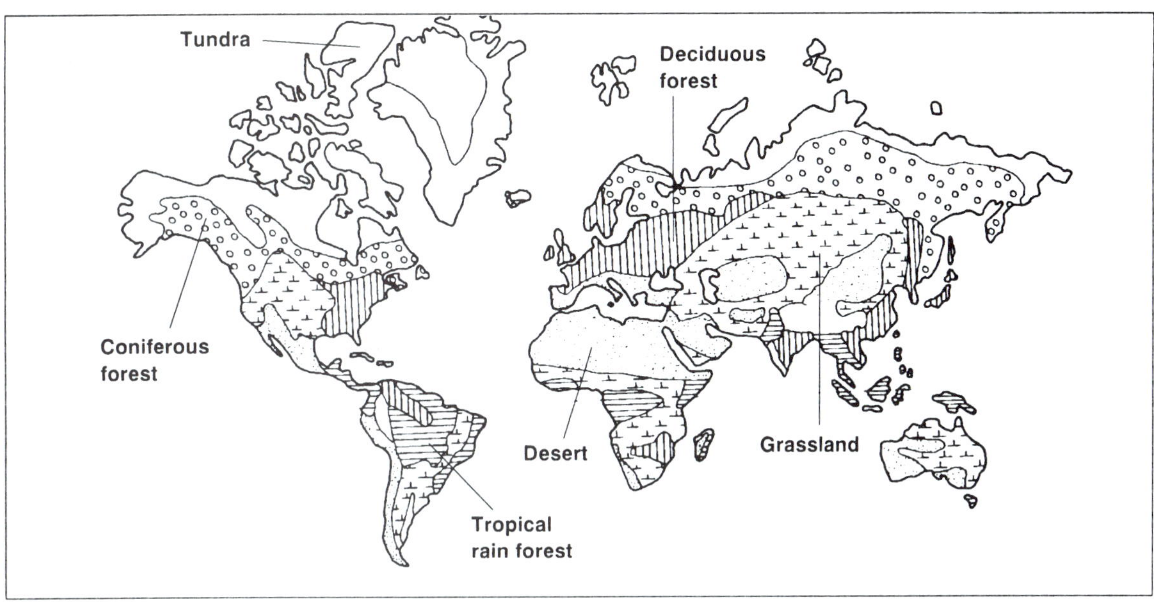

Figure A

1. In which biome do you live? ______________________________

COMPARING BIOMES

The chart below shows the climates of the major land biomes. Study the chart and then answer the questions.

BIOME	AVERAGE YEARLY RAINFALL	AVERAGE YEARLY TEMPERATURE RANGE
Tundra	less than 25 cm	-25°C-4°C
Coniferous forest	35-75 cm	-10°C-14°C
Deciduous forest	75-125 cm	6°C-28°C
Tropical rain forest	200-450 cm	25°C-28°C
Grassland	25-75 cm	0°C-25°C
Desert	less than 25 cm	24°C-40°C

2. What is the average yearly temperature range of the tropical rain forest biome?

____

3. What biome gets between 75 and 125 cm of rainfall per year? ____________________

WHAT DO THE PICTURES SHOW?

The photographs show the six major land biomes. Identify each biome. Write the name of the correct biome on the line below each photograph.

Figure B

1. This photograph shows a

    ________________ biome.

Figure C

2. This photograph shows a

    ________________ biome.

Figure D

3. This photograph shows a

    ________________ biome.

Figure E

4. This photograph shows a

    ________________ biome.

Figure F

5. This photograph shows a

_______________ biome.

Figure G

6. This photograph shows a

_______________ biome.

MULTIPLE CHOICE

In the space provided, write the letter of the word that best complete each statement.

_________ 1. Permafrost occurs in

a) deserts. b) the tundra.

c) coniferous forests. d) tropical rain forests.

_________ 2. Trees such as pines and firs make up

a) tropical rain forests. b) the tundra.

c) coniferous forests. d) grasslands.

_________ 3. The biome which supports more plant and animal species than any other is the

a) tropical rain forest. b) deciduous forest.

c) coniferous forest. d) grasslands.

_________ 4. Very few animals can survive in

a) tropical rain forests. b) deserts.

c) grasslands. d) deciduous forests.

_________ 5. Trees that shed their leaves in the fall make up

a) the tundra. b) coniferous forests.

c) grasslands. d) deciduous forests.

COMPLETE THE CHART

Study the characteristics of land biomes in the chart below. Complete the chart by placing a check mark in the correct column.

Land Biomes								
	Characteristics	**Tundra**	**Coniferous forest**	**Desert**	**Deciduous forest**	**Grassland**	**Tropical rain forest**
1.	Very hot days and very cool nights						
2.	Trees with needle shaped leaves grow						
3.	Used as farmland						
4.	Hot and wet all year						
5.	Permafrost						
6.	Maple and oak tree grow						
7.	Cacti grow						
8.	Spruce and moose are common						
9.	Wheat and corn grow						
10.	Jungles						
11.	Trees lose leaves in fall						
12.	Conifers grow						
13.	Reindeer live						

What things can change the environment?

23

succession [suk-SESH-un]: process by which populations in an ecosystem are replaced by new populations

LESSON 23 What things can change the environment?

One of the world's greatest disasters took place on August 27, 1883. A volcano on the island of Krakatoa exploded. Much of the island was blown to bits. One part that had stood almost a kilometer high, was left covered by nearly 275 meters of water.

The explosion caused a huge tidal wave. It swept over nearby islands. More than 36,000 people drowned.

The Krakatoa disaster caused great changes in the environment. Volcanic dust soared high into the atmosphere. Much of the sun's energy was blocked. Winds carried this dust around the world for more than a year. Temperatures dropped. Crops did not grow well. Animals were confused. They could not tell day from night.

Earth's history is a history of change. Some changes, like the Krakatoa volcano, earthquakes, lightning-caused fires. severe storms, floods, and droughts, are natural events. Events change the environment. When the environment changes, its populations are slowly replaced by new populations. This process is called **succession**. [suk-SESH-un].

A change in one group of organisms causes a change in another group. Changes first occur in plant populations. Then, different animals move in.

A STORY OF DESTRUCTION AND REBIRTH

Each year, more than four million acres of American forests are destroyed by fire.

Most of the plant life is destroyed. Many animals die; others flee.

Figure A

Nothing is left but ashes and black skeletons of what were once living trees.

The forest community is gone.... But it will not stay that way. Many changes will take place to restore the forest. But it will take many years....

Figure B

1. First, grasses and weeds grow. They grow from roots and seeds left in the soil. They grow well. There are no trees to block the sunlight.

Figure C

2. These plants mature and form seeds. The wind spreads the seeds. Soon, a meadow forms. Small animals, like insects and birds, return to the area.

Figure D

3. Many growing seasons pass. The weeds, grasses, and insects add minerals to the soil. The soil becomes richer.

Figure E

4. The soil can support shrubs and small, fast-growing woody trees. These plants block the sun from the grasses and weeds. Other plants, like ferns, do not need full sunlight. They grow where the grasses and weeds once were. Different kinds of animals move in.

Figure F

5. The soil becomes richer. Taller, slower-growing hardwood trees grow. Other animals move in, such as rabbits, chipmunks, squirrels, and deer.

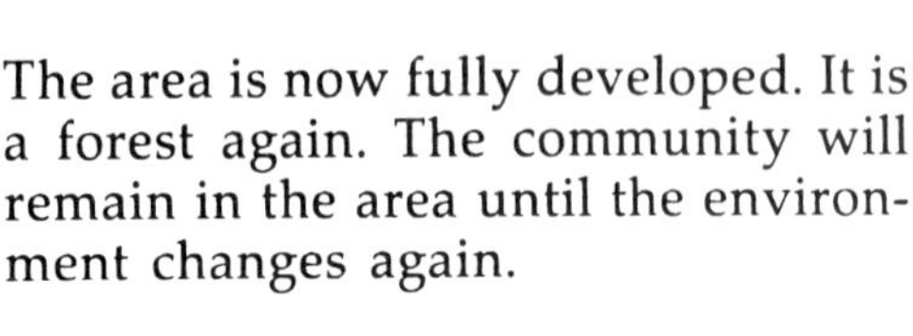

The area is now fully developed. It is a forest again. The community will remain in the area until the environment changes again.

Figure G

FILL IN THE BLANK

Complete each statement using a term or terms from the list below. Write your answers in the spaces provided.

trees	changing	succession
shrubs	animals	hardwood
plant	slow	grasses
natural	weeds	

1. The earth is always ______________ .
2. A slow change in populations of organisms in an area is called ______________ .
3. In succession, the first changes occur in ______________ populations.
4. If a forest burns down, ______________ and ______________ are the first to grow.
5. When plant populations change, different ______________ move in.
6. Changes such as volcanos and earthquakes are ______________ events.
7. Oak and maple trees are most likely to be found in a ______________ forest.
8. As seasons pass, grasses and weeds are replaced by ______________ .
9. Succession is a ______________ process.
10. Grasses and weeds grow well when there are no ______________ to block the sunlight.

REACHING OUT

The steps below describe the destruction and rebuilding of a forest ecosystem. Place the steps in the proper order.

- shrubs and fast-growing short trees
- chipmunks and rabbits
- meadow
- dead forest
- grasses and weeds
- small birds and insects
- forest
- fire
- slow-growing, tall hardwood trees

1. ____________________
2. ____________________
3. ____________________
4. ____________________
5. ____________________
6. ____________________
7. ____________________
8. ____________________
9. ____________________

How do people upset the balance of nature?

24

pollutants [puh-LOOT-ents]: harmful substances
pollution [puh-LOO-shun]: anything that harms the environment

LESSON 24 | How do people upset the balance of nature?

An environment is constantly changing. Sometimes, the changes work together to keep the environment in balance. In a balanced environment, the size of the population remains about the same over time.

Sometimes the balance in an environment is upset. Many times people upset the balance of nature. People upset the balance of nature by destroying the habitats of other living things. For example, people cut down forests for farms and towns. They build dams and dig mines. All of these human activities can be harmful to other organisms in the environment. Many species of animals are finding it hard to survive because of the ways people have upset the balance of nature.

People also upset the balance of nature by causing **pollution** [puh-LOO-shun]. You probably know that pollution is a major problem. Pollution is <u>anything</u> that harms the environment. It occurs when harmful substances, or **pollutants** [puh-LOOT-ents] are released into the environment. Pollution of the air, land, and water are all major problems. Today many different substances are poisoning the environment and upsetting nature's balance. And we cannot think of <u>just</u> air pollution, or <u>just</u> water pollution, or <u>just</u> land pollution. Pollution may <u>start out</u> in one part of our environment. <u>But it does not remain there</u>. It S-P-R-E-A-D-S to all parts.

Pollution is increasing daily. Like other organisms, people also suffer from the effects of pollution - in the form of illness, birth defects, respiratory diseases, and many other problems. Therefore, we must all work together to help reduce pollution.

AIR POLLUTION

Study the pictures below and read the text describing each picture then answer the questions.

Figure A

The burning of fossil fuels is the major cause of air pollution. Oil, coal, and natural gas are fossil fuels. When these fuels are burned, many harmful substances are released into the air.

1. How do you think car-pooling helps reduce air pollution? ______________

____

____

Figure B

When some harmful gasses are released into the air, they combine with water to form acids. The acids fall to the earth as <u>acid</u> <u>rain</u>. Acid rain kills living things. It also damages buildings and statues.

2. What is acid rain? ______________

____

____

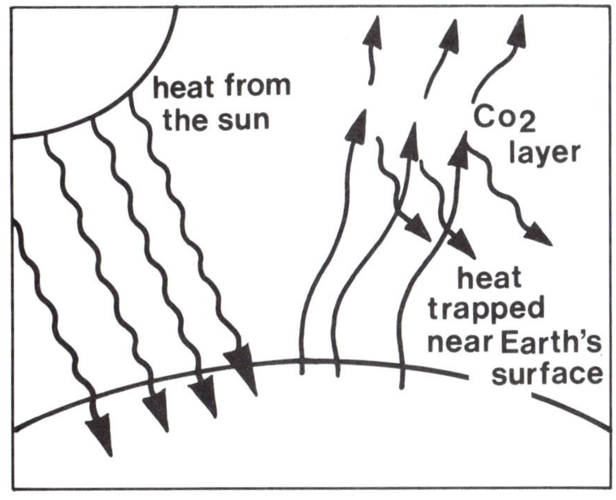

Figure C

Fuels need oxygen when they burn. They give off carbon dioxide. Carbon dioxide traps heat energy from the sun.

3. Scientists think that the increase of carbon dioxide in the air is causing the temperature of the earth to

______________________________ .
rise, fall

WATER AND LAND POLLUTION

Water pollution occurs when harmful substances enter the water. Major sources of water pollution include sewage, chemical wastes from factories, and fertilizers [FUR-tul-y-zuhrs], and pesticides [PES-tuh-sides] washed off farm fields.

You have probably seen cans, bottles, and papers thrown on the ground. These thrown-away materials are called litter. Litter is one cause of land pollution. Garbage and chemical wastes are other sources of land pollution. We produce billions of tons of garbage each year. Chemical wastes are often buried in the ground.

NOW TRY THIS!

Ten pollutants and pollutant sources are listed below.

Write **water** next to those that start out as water pollution. Write **land** next to those that start out as land pollution.

_________ **1.** raw sewage discharge

_________ **2.** dumping of chemicals into rivers

_________ **3.** pesticides

_________ **4.** detergents

_________ **5.** garbage

_________ **6.** burial of drums of toxic wastes

_________ **7.** fertilizers

_________ **8.** use of DDT to control mosquitos

_________ **9.** litter

_________ **10.** abandoning junk cars

Explain how a pollutant gas in the atmosphere can become

a) water pollution ____

____

b) land pollution ____

____

FILL IN THE BLANK

Complete each statement using a term or terms from the list below. Write your answers in the spaces provided.

spreads	illness	air
pollution	balanced	reduce
sun	does not	defects
sewage	survive	wastes
pollutants		

1. Anything that harms the environment is ______________ .
2. Pollution occurs when ______________ enter the environment.
3. The size of a population remains about the same in a ______________ environment.
4. Many species are finding it hard to ______________ because of human activity.
5. Major sources of water pollution include ______________ and chemical ______________ .
6. Pollution can cause ______________ and birth ______________ in people.
7. Pollution ______________ stay in one place. It ______________ to all parts of the environment.
8. To help nature maintain a proper balance, we must ______________ pollution.
9. The burning of fossil fuels is the major cause of ______________ pollution.
10. Carbon dioxide traps energy from the ______________ .

REACHING OUT

About <u>66,000 square miles</u> of the world's tropical rain forests are being destroyed each year. How does this upset the balance of nature? ______________________________

____

SCIENCE *EXTRA*

Wildlife Refuge Manager

How would you go about saving animals and plants? You could become a wildlife refuge manager. A wildlife refuge manager supervises a protected area for wild plants and animals. Refuges may be in forests, deserts, wetlands, or other habitats.

In order to properly protect plants and animals, refuge managers need to understand how the weather and soil affect living things. So they often measure temperature, rainfall, and soil chemistry. Refuge mangers also work with the plants and animals directly. They count the numbers of different species living in the refuge. This is called taking a census. It is important for managers to know the population sizes of wildlife species they are trying to protect. Sometimes, however, there are so many plants or animals of one kind that it is impossible to count them all. In this case, managers estimate population size from a sample. This means that they count individual plants or animals in a small area, then compare the sample area to the size of the refuge.

Sometimes, refuge mangers take active steps to protect a rare plant or animal. If a refuge contains a rare species of bird, for example, the manager might keep visitors away from all nesting places, or close the refuge during the nesting season.

You need a bachelor's degree in biology, botany, or zoology to become a wildlife refuge manger. Preparing reports and analyzing data from the field also are part of the manager's job. So it is helpful to study mathematics, statistics, and technical writing as preparation for this career. You should also enjoy outdoor work, including working in the rain, snow, heat, or cold. Refuge managers sometimes must be out in bad weather, because protecting wildlife cannot always wait for a warm sunny day.

What is conservation? 25

conservation [kon-sur-VAY-shun]: wise use of natural resources
natural resources: materials and energy in the biosphere that are used by living things
nonrenewable resources: resources that cannot be replaced
renewable resources: resources that can be replaced by nature

LESSON 25 What is conservation?

Think about your pantry. It contains many kinds of foods. When they run low, you replace them. But what if you knew that you could not replace certain items? What would you do?

You would try to make them last as long as possible. You would use them sparingly, or conserve them. Conserve means to protect from being used up.

Earth is like a huge pantry. It has all the things we need to stay alive. It is also stocked with things that modern people use, like ores for metals and fuels for energy. All of the things we get from the environment are called **natural resources**.

There are two main groups of natural resources, renewable resources and nonrenewable resources.

RENEWABLE RESOURCES are replaced by nature. Oxygen, water, soil, and living things are renewable resources. Oxygen is made by plants during photosynthesis. Soil is made when rocks break up. Water is renewed through the water cycle. Living things reproduce themselves

NONRENEWABLE RESOURCES are not replaced by nature, at least, not in a reasonable period of time. Fossil fuels, such as oil, coal and natural gas are nonrenewable resources so are minerals. We get metals from mineral ores. How would your life be different without fossil fuels and metals?

At one time our supply of natural resources seemed endless. Now, we know differently. The population of the world is increasing. We are using more, wasting more, and polluting more natural resources than we did in the past.

Earth's "pantry" is limited. We must use our resources wisely. If we do not, there will not be enough resources left for future generations.

AREAS OF CONSERVATION

The wise use of our natural resources is called **conservation** [kon-sur-VAY-shun]. Conservation of all natural resources, including renewable resources is important. Even though renewable resources are replaced, their supply is limited. People must be careful not to use them up faster than they can be replaced.

AIR CONSERVATION

Air pollution is very bad in most industrial areas and cities. But, air pollution spreads everywhere. It reaches every place on Earth.

Polluted air can smell bad. It can cause health problems, like respiratory diseases, lung cancer, and allergies. Polluted air also kills trees and reduces food crops.

Motor vehicles and factories are the major causes of air pollution. Strict laws concerning air pollution must be passed and enforced.

Figure A

What laws would you suggest to help cut down on air pollution. ____________________

____

One of the least expensive ways to control air pollution is to walk instead of drive and use public transportation.

WATER CONSERVATION

The average person drinks about 228 gallons of water each year. But water is not only used for drinking. We use it in many other ways. For example we use water for bathing, swimming, cleaning, cooking, gardening, and boating. Water is also vital for proper sewage disposal, industry, agriculture, and aquaculture.

Our water supply must be kept fresh and safe to drink. We must stop dumping wastes and raw sewage into our water supply. We can also conserve water by turning off the water when brushing teeth and taking showers instead of baths.

Figure B

What other ways can you conserve water? ____________________________________

____

SOIL CONSERVATION

It takes nature from 500 to 1000 years to produce about two and one-half centimeters (one inch) of topsoil.

Soil can be carried away by wind and moving water. This removal of soil is called erosion. Erosion can be reduced.

To prevent to much soil erosion, people must practice soil conservation.

Figure C

Some ways to conserve soil are:

a) Cover the soil with plants such as grass or shrubs. The roots of plants help hold soil together.

b) Restrict the cutting down of forests. Trees act as a wind breaks and help prevent soil from being blown away by wind.

c) Plant crops across the slope of a hill instead of up and down the hill. This helps prevent soil from being carried away by water running down the hill.

d) Add materials like humus or natural fertilizers to the soil.

Figure D

WILDLIFE CONSERVATION

All the natural plants and animals living in an area are called **wildlife**. Wildlife are part of nature. They provide us with food, clothes, and many other products. Wildlife are also pretty to look at.

Figure E

Human activity can cause many forms of wildlife to become extinct (die out). We pollute and overhunt. We destroy wildlife habitats for construction and mining. These actions disturb nature's balance.

Some methods of wildlife conservation are:

a) Protecting the habitats of organisms.

b) Enforcing strict hunting and fishing laws.

c) Setting aside refuges, parks, and other public lands for wildlife.

d) Providing special "breeding grounds" for endangered (organisms in danger of becoming extinct) species.

Forests are "home" for many plants and animals. Forests provide us with oxygen, lumber, wood pulp, medicines, and many other products. Wood pulp used to make paper, including the pages of this book.

Tropical rain forests have more plant and animal species than any other place on earth.

Many of the habitats being lost are in the tropical rain forests.

Figure F

Fires caused by human carelessness destroy many forests. Public education about dangers of forest fires is one way to help conserve forests.

Other methods of forest conservation include:

a) Planting new trees to replace those that have been chopped down for lumber or other products.

b) Chopping down only certain parts of a forest to allow seeds from remaining trees to provide replacements.

c) Removing only older or unhealthy trees from forest regions.

Figure G

METAL CONSERVATION

To recycle means to "use over again." Some resources, like metals, can be recycled. Aluminum cans, glass bottles, newspapers and some of the metals used to make cars can all be recycled. They can be melted down and reused. Most can be recycled over and over again. Recycling is an important way to conserve minerals.

Figure H

FUEL CONSERVATION

Fuels are nonrenewable resources. Once a fuel is used, it is gone. It cannot be recycled. The best way to conserve a fuel is not to waste it. Use it sparingly. Use it as you would a nonreplaceable item in your pantry.

Here are some ways people can help conserve fuel.

a) Use cars that get good gas mileage. Drive the speed limit.
b) Walk, bicycle, or car pool when possible.
c) Turn off lights when you leave a room. This saves the fuel used to produce electricity.
d) Use electrical appliances that are energy saving.

MULTIPLE CHOICE

In the space provided, write the letter of the word that best completes each statement.

_____ 1. All the things nature gives are called.

a) pantries b) ores
c) natural resources d) renewable resources

_____ 2. The things that nature replaces in a short period of time are called

a) renewable resources b) nonrenewable resources
c) fossil fuels d) wildlife

_____ 3. An example of a renewable resource is

a) coal b) aluminum ore
c) oxygen d) oil

_____ 4. Things that nature does not replace in a reasonable period of time are called

a) renewable resources b) nonrenewable resources
c) pollution d) natural resources

_____ 5. An example of a non renewable resource is

a) water b) soil
c) air d) minerals

_____ 6. The wise use of our natural resources is called

a) recycling b) consideration
c) conservation d) erosion

_____ 7. Organisms in danger of dying off are considered

a) endangered b) extinct
c) conserved d) wildlife

_____ 8. The use of resources over and over again is called

a) erosion b) cycling
c) recycling d) replacement

MATCHING

Match each term in Column A with its description in Column B. Write the correct letter in the space provided.

	Column A	Column B
________	1. water, air, soil and living things	a) wise use of resources
________	2. minerals and fossil fuels	b) cause of most pollution
________	3. conservation	c) non renewable resource
________	4. pollution	d) renewable resource
________	5. people	e) harms all living things

REACHING OUT

Make a list of five things you use often. Identify the natural resource (or resources) that each of the things you listed came from.

ITEM	NATURAL RESOURCE (S)
________________	________________
________________	________________
________________	________________
________________	________________
________________	________________

THE METRIC SYSTEM

METRIC-ENGLISH CONVERSIONS

	Metric to English	*English to Metric*
Length	1 kilometer = 0.621 mile (mi)	1 mi = 1.61 km
	1 meter = 3.28 feet (ft)	1 ft = 0.305 m
	1 centimeter = 0.394 inch (in)	1 in = 2.54 cm
Area	1 square meter = 10.763 square feet	1 ft^2 = 0.0929 m^2
	1 square centimeter = 0.155 square inch	1 in^2 = 6.452 cm^2
Volume	1 cubic meter = 35.315 cubic feet	1 ft^3 = 0.0283 m^3
	1 cubic centimeter = 0.0610 cubic inches	1 in^3 = 16.39 cm^3
	1 liter = .2642 gallon (gal)	1 gal = 3.79 L
	1 liter = 1.06 quart (qt)	1 qt = 0.94 L
Mass	1 kilogram = 2.205 pound (lb)	1 lb = 0.4536 kg
	1 gram = 0.0353 ounce (oz)	1 oz = 28.35 g
Temperature	Celsius = 5/9 (°F –32)	Fahrenheit = 9/5°C + 32
	0°C = 32°F (Freezing point of water)	72°F = 22°C (Room temperature)
	100°C = 212°F (Boiling point of water)	98.6°F = 37°C (Human body temperature)

METRIC UNITS

The basic unit is printed in capital letters.

Length	*Symbol*
Kilometer	km
METER	m
centimeter	cm
millimeter	mm
Area	*Symbol*
square kilometer	km^2
SQUARE METER	m^2
square millimeter	mm^2
Volume	*Symbol*
CUBIC METER	m^3
cubic millimeter	mm^3
liter	L
milliliter	mL
Mass	*Symbol*
KILOGRAM	kg
gram	g
Temperature	*Symbol*
degree Celsius	°C

SOME COMMON METRIC PREFIXES

Prefix		*Meaning*
micro-	=	0.000001, or 1 / 1,000,000
milli-	=	0.001, or 1 / 1000
centi-	=	0.01, or 1 / 100
deci-	=	0.1, or 1 / 10
deka-	=	10
hecto-	=	100
kilo-	=	1000
mega-	=	1,000,000

SOME METRIC RELATIONSHIPS

Unit	*Relationship*
kilometer	1 km = 1000 m
meter	1 m = 100 cm
centimeter	1 cm = 10 mm
millimeter	1 mm = 0.1 cm
liter	1 L = 1000 mL
milliliter	1 mL = 0.001 L
tonne	1 t = 1000 kg
kilogram	1 kg = 1000 g
gram	1 g = 1000 mg
centigram	1 cg = 10 mg
milligram	1 mg = 0.001 g

GLOSSARY/INDEX

adaptation [ad-up-TAY-shun]: trait of an organism that helps it live in its environment, 73
AIDS: viral disease that attacks a person immune system, 101
anatomy [uh-NAT-uh-mee]: study of the parts, or structures, of living things, 65
anthropologists [an-thruh-PAHL-uh-jists]: scientists who study human beings and trace their evolution, 85
antibiotic [an-ti-by-AHT-ik]: chemical substances that kill harmful bacteria, 125
antibodies [AN-ti-bahd-eez]: proteins made by the body that destroy germs, 117

biomes [BY-ohms]: large region of the earth that has characteristic kinds of organisms, 141
biosphere [BY-uh-sfir]: thin zone of the earth that supports all life, 129
bipedal [by-PEED-uhl]: upright; walk on two legs instead of four, 79
blending: combination of genes in which a mixture of both traits shows, 27

camouflage [KAM-uh-flahj]: ability of an organism to blend in with its surroundings, 73
capsid [KAP-sid]: coat of protein that covers a virus, 95
chromosome [KROH-muh-sohm]: threadlike structures in the nucleus of a cell that control heredity, 7
cilia [SIL-ee-uh]: tiny hairlike structures, 117
cloning: production of organisms with identical genes, 53
community: all the organisms living in a certain area, 129
conservation [kon-sur-VAY-shun]: wise use of natural resources, 159
consumers [kun-SOO-murs]: organisms that get food by eating other organisms, 133
contagious [kuhn-TAY-jus] **disease:** infectious disease that can be transmitted from person to person, 101
controlled breeding: mating organisms to produce offspring with certain traits, 47

decomposers [dee-kum-POHZ-ers]: organisms that feed on dead organisms, 133
dominant [DOM-uh-nunt] **gene:** stronger gene that always shows itself, 15

ecology [ee-KAHL-uh-jee]: study of the relationship between living things and their environment, 129
ecosystem [EE-koh-sis-tum]: all the living things and nonliving parts of an environment, 129
evolution [ev-uh-LOO-shun]: process by which organisms change over time, 59
extinct: organism that no longer exists on earth, 59

fossils: remains of organisms that lived in the past, 59

gamete: sex cell, 7
gene: part of a chromosome that controls inherited traits, 7
gene splicing [SPLYS-ing]: moving a section of DNA from the genes of one organism to the genes of another organism, 53
genetic engineering [juh-NET-ik en-juh-NEER-ing]: methods used to produce new forms of DNA, 53
genetics [juh-NET-iks]: study of heredity, 7

habitat [HAB-i-tat]: place where an organism lives, 133
hominids [HOM-uh-nids]: group of primates in which modern humans and their ancestors are classified, 85
hybrid [HY-brid]: having two unlike genes, 15
hybridization [hy-brid-ih-ZAY-shun]: mating two different kinds of organisms, 47

immune system: body system made up of cells and tissues that help a person fight disease, 101

immunity [im-MYOON-i-tee]: resistance to a certain disease, 117
inbreeding: mating closely related organisms, 47
incomplete dominance: blending of traits carried by two or more different genes, 27
infectious [in-FEK-shus] **disease:** disease caused when a virus (or germs) enter the body, 101

mass selection: crossing organisms with desirable traits, 47
mimicry [MIM-ik-ree]: adaptation of an organism that protects the organism because its appearance is similar to another organism, 73
mucus [MYOU-kus]: sticky substance that traps germs, 117

natural resources: materials and energy in the biosphere that are used by living things, 159
natural selection: survival of organisms with favorable traits, 59
niche [NICH]: an organism's role, or job, in its environment, 133
noninfectious diseases: diseases that are not caused by germs and not spread from person to person, 109
nonrenewable resources: resources that cannot be replaced, 159
nucleic [new-KLEE-ik] **acids:** organic compounds that make proteins, control the cell, and determine heredity, 95

opposable thumb: a thumb that can touch all of the other fingers, 79

pollutants [puh-LOOT-ents]: harmful substances, 153
pollution [puh-LOO-shun]: anything that harms the environment, 153
population: all the members of one species that live in the same area, 129
primates: order of mammals, 79
producers: organisms that can make their own food, 133
Punnett square: chart used to show possible gene combinations, 21
pure: having two like genes, 15

recessive [ri-SES-iv] **gene:** weaker gene that is hidden when the dominant gene is present, 15
renewable resources: resources that can be replaced by nature, 159

sex chromosomes: X and Y chromosomes, 35
succession [suk-SESH-un]: process by which populations in an ecosystem are replaced by new populations, 147

toxins: poisons, 101
traits: characteristics of living things, 1

vestigial [ves-TIJ-ee-uhl] **structures:** body parts that are reduced in size and that serve no function, 65
virus: piece of nucleic acid covered with an outercoat of protein, 95

white blood cells: cells that protect the body against disease, 117